DEAN SMITH
A BIOGRAPHY

DEAN SMITH
A BIOGRAPHY

by Thad Mumau

JOHN F. BLAIR, PUBLISHER
WINSTON-SALEM, NORTH CAROLINA

LIBRARY OF CONGRESS CATALOGING-IN-PUBLICATION DATA

Mumau, Thad.
Dean Smith : A biography / by Thad Mumau.
p.   cm.
Rev. ed. of: The Dean Smith story. c1980.
ISBN 0-89587-080-0 (alk. paper)
1. Smith, Dean, 1931–   . 2. Basketball—United States—Coaches-
-Biography.   3. University of North Carolina at Chapel Hill-
-Basketball.   I. Mumau, Thad. Dean Smith story.   II. Title.
GV884.S54M85   1990
796.323'092—dc20
[B]
90-41878

With much love—
to my wife and wonderful friend, Dahlia
and to our daughters, Erika and Laura.
You all make me feel very fortunate.

TABLE OF CONTENTS

Foreword by Michael Jordan   ix

Acknowledgments   xiii

THE HOUSE THAT DEAN BUILT   3

LOOKING BACK   15

THE EARLY YEARS   34

TWENTY-FOUR-CARAT GOLD   61

A DECADE OF DOMINANCE   94

THE LITTLE THINGS   128

THE SMITH BLUEPRINT   148

ISSUES AND ANSWERS   166

MORE THAN A COACH—WHAT THE PLAYERS SAY   177

PRAISE FROM PEERS   217

INSIDE DEAN SMITH   250

Appendix   275

Michael Jordan

Photo by Hugh Morton

FOREWORD

Coach Smith has meant so much to me. In a way, I owe my success to him. He taught me many, many things, and not just about basketball.

I always tell people that I have been fortunate to be part of a family which is very close. My mother and father taught me right from wrong and about true values in life. Then I had Dean Smith for my college coach, and he taught me more of the same things. Besides being the best coach there is, he was more—kind of a coach-father type.

My three years at Carolina were wonderful years, and in terms of basketball, that was because of Coach Smith. He was always teaching. And if you listened to what he was saying, he was teaching things that would be important off the basketball court, too.

I was a North Carolina State fan before I met Coach Smith and visited Chapel Hill. But after talking to him, I knew Carolina was where I wanted to go. He doesn't promise you anything, except that you'll have the chance to get a good education. In fact, he makes it clear that getting a degree is what he emphasizes first.

I was always impressed with the way Coach would be teaching, always teaching. He didn't leave anything uncovered. We learned fundamentals I had never thought about. When I got to the NBA, I knew how to play basketball. Every player doesn't really know all of the little things about the game, but Carolina players do because Dean Smith teaches those things. When I got to the NBA—even though I had only played three years of college ball—I was totally prepared. There was nothing that came up in practice that Coach Smith hadn't taught me. Every year in drills, we go over things that Coach was teaching right from the start. Boxing out, getting over screens, defensive position—I learned it all from him.

But when I look back, the fact that Coach cared about me and all of my teammates as people more than as basketball players is what means the most. He would sit down and talk with me about school and about life. A lot is said, I guess, about the positive image I have, and that's important to me. I really want to be a good role model for youngsters. I'm careful to be that.

Some people wonder how I resist a lot of the stuff that's going on—drugs, drinking, parties that end up with trouble—and I tell them that my mother and Dean Smith told me an easy way to avoid all that: when you find yourself in a situation that could be potential trouble, leave that situation. Just leave. I've done that, along with just not going some places I knew could possibly be bad.

I remember when I turned pro. I didn't really want to do it. I was having fun at Carolina and wanted to stay for my senior year. Coach Smith showed me why I shouldn't stay, why I couldn't afford not to go into the NBA after my junior year. A lot of coaches would never do that; they would be thinking about the next season and themselves. I wasn't surprised that Coach Smith actually talked me into going pro, though, because he is not selfish. He is always thinking of his players, even after they're not his players anymore.

He's meant a lot to me. And you know, when I'm playing and Coach is at the game, I still think about pleasing him. I want to play that good defense, because I know that's what he likes.

Dean Smith is a good friend.

Michael Jordan

ACKNOWLEDGMENTS

Anyone who writes a book probably hears that it's quite an accomplishment. There are many people who share in that accomplishment, as is certainly the case with me and my endeavor to tell the story of Dean Smith's life.

There is no way I could have gone back into Smith's boyhood without the excellent help I received from his mother and father and his sister, Joan. They were always willing to share memories and to provide interesting anecdotes.

Linda Woods, the administrative secretary of the North Carolina basketball office, was a strong right hand throughout the process of gathering information. She was always helpful, always cheerful in opening doors I couldn't otherwise have entered.

Rick Brewer and the UNC Sports Information Department found time to dig out pictures and go back into the past for details. In shooting pictures of Tar Heel basketball games for parts of five decades, Hugh Morton has captured large chunks of Smith's life on film, and he graciously contributed his genius to this book. Ken Cooke and the *Fayetteville Observer-Times* photography staff also provided shots of some of the Carolina coach's greatest moments and players.

The UNC basketball players themselves were terrific. Their loyalty was apparent as they talked about their relationship with Smith and what it was like to play for him.

Speaking of relationships, I have had a tremendous one with my publisher. Margaret Couch, Carolyn Sakowski, and Steve Kirk have made what has been an enjoyable experience even more enjoyable. I also owe thanks to David Perry, who helped get John F. Blair, Publisher, and me together.

The friendship of Samuel Guy, John Campbell, and Ron Sellers has meant more to me than I can say. No one could be a better friend than Gary Fleck. Dennis Wuycik, whom I once covered as a Tar Heel all-American, is a kind employer and an even kinder friend. His encouragement was invaluable to this project.

My dad and mom taught me early what Dean Smith has always emphasized to his players: that competition in sports is great, but the only truly important result in anything is knowing you gave your top effort. It was Mom who inspired me to write Dean Smith's story. She spent long and tireless hours as my chief editor, and I miss her now that she is gone. My sister, Judy, has always been there for me.

And there have been so many others—Sue Teague, Loyd Auman, Dwight Miller, and Margaret and George Perkins among them.

Finally, I thank Dean Smith for the opportunity to be the author of his biography. He's every bit the wonderful person he is portrayed to be.

I've been very lucky to have folks like all of those mentioned here to help me. Thanks.

DEAN SMITH
A BIOGRAPHY

THE HOUSE THAT DEAN BUILT

Dean Smith. The name of the University of North Carolina basketball coach has become so indelibly stamped onto college basketball that it is practically part of the game itself. In Chapel Hill, an Ivy League–style college town, he is larger than life. Indeed, the man is regarded as a legend not only by Tar Heel fans but throughout college basketball. His record speaks for itself. He is closing in on 700 career wins, and his teams make National Collegiate Athletic Association Tournament participation a habit.

It wasn't always that way. In fact, there was a time early in Smith's career at Carolina—the only place he's ever served as head coach—when a group of students tried to hoot him off campus. Never one to be influenced by either criticism or praise, Smith endured and excelled, and he now owns the town. Over his 29-year stay in the college game, he has also practically owned the Atlantic Coast Conference, considered one of the nation's strongest leagues year in and year out.

Smith is so beloved in the state of North Carolina that some in the political arena feel he would be a cinch to be elected to the United States Senate. He is so highly respected by his peers that a poll of the country's college basketball coaches named him the best. Many members of the coaching fraternity point to the Tar Heel coach's record, his teaching ability, the graduation rate of his players, and his impact on the game over the course of three decades.

Smith's Carolina teams have won more than three-fourths of their games—most of them against the nation's toughest competition. There was a National Invitation Tournament title in 1971 and an NCAA championship in 1982. Smith has won more than twice as many ACC championships, both tournament and regular season, as any other coach in league history. Smith also received the honor of guiding the United States team to the gold medal in basketball in the 1976 Olympics.

Those are just some of the reasons Smith was given the ultimate tribute by the University of North Carolina in 1986, when the school's spectacular basketball and entertainment complex opened its doors and held its dedication. While several names for the complex were tossed about, only one was considered truly appropriate.

Carmichael Auditorium was inadequate for Carolina basketball almost before its construction was completed. Although its cozy confines provided one of the college game's greatest home-court advantages (a UNC record of 168–20), the arena was simply too small. The success of Smith's teams swelled the Tar Heel following to such proportions that by 1965, when Carmichael opened, demand for tickets far exceeded supply. Talk of a new place for North Carolina to play began.

The entire cost of building a complex to replace Carmichael was met by private donations. Contributions came from over 2,300 individuals and ranged from $1 to $1 million. It took only six years to raise $33.8 million, an amazing feat that can be attributed to the program built by Smith.

Inside the Smith Center

Photo by Hugh Morton

The ACC has long been one of the best-balanced and strongest conferences in college basketball. No other league has surpassed it over the past few decades. Fans educated down to the fine print on the subject of roundball point to the ACC for its consistency in beating fine nonconference opposition and for representation among national top-20 polls. North Carolina has taken up permanent residence in these rankings; through the end of the eighties, the Tar Heels finished in the top 10 nine straight years and 15 of the previous 16. Smith's teams won 25 or more games nine successive seasons, from 1981 to 1989, and 17 times overall, and they have won 20 or more for 20 consecutive years, 23 times overall.

As for the ACC, where coaching genius is no stranger, Smith has been king. Carolina under Smith has not had a losing record in the conference in 26 years. Each of the other seven ACC members has finished last in the standings at least once during that period, while UNC has placed no worse than third. That demonstrates the kind of dominance Smith's teams have enjoyed. In addition, they have finished first (or tied for the top spot) 15 times. The coach closest in first-place finishes is Frank McGuire, with six.

Magnifying Smith's success in the ACC is the fact that three other outstanding coaches did not approach his glowing achievements. Everett Case, the man credited with bringing basketball fever from Indiana to Dixie, founded a dynasty at North Carolina State. He won four ACC Tournament championships. Vic Bubas established Duke as a national power in the early and middle years of the 1960s. He also won four ACC titles. Frank McGuire took North Carolina to the national championship in 1957 and coached South Carolina to prominence in the ACC. He won two league tournaments. Smith's Tar Heels have claimed 10.

That a team could win more than 80 percent of its games against formidable competition for any length of time in college basketball is almost unfathomable. That's exactly what Smith-coached Carolina teams have done, though, reeling off

Dean Smith's Career at North Carolina

Year	W-L	Pct.	ACC W-L	ACC Finish	ACC Tournament	Final National Poll Finishes	Post-Season
1961-62	8-9	.471	7-7	Tied 4th	Quarterfinals		
1962-63	15-6	.714	10-4	Third	Semifinals		
1963-64	12-12	.500	6-8	Fifth	Semifinals		
1964-65	15-9	.625	10-4	Tied 2nd	Quarterfinals		
1965-66	16-11	.593	8-6	Third	Semifinals		
1966-67	26-6	.813	12-2	First	Champion	3rd AP, 4th UPI	NCAA 4th Place
1967-68	28-4	.875	12-2	First	Champion	4th AP, 3rd UPI	NCAA Runner-up
1968-69	27-5	.844	12-2	First	Champion	4th AP, 2nd UPI	NCAA 4th Place
1969-70	18-9	.667	9-5	Tied 2nd	Quarterfinals		NIT First Round
1970-71	26-6	.813	11-3	First	Finalist	13th AP & UPI	NIT Champion
1971-72	26-5	.839	9-3	First	Champion	2nd AP & UPI	NCAA 3rd Place
1972-73	25-8	.758	8-4	Second	Quarterfinals	11th AP, 12th UPI	NIT 3rd Place
1973-74	22-6	.786	9-3	Tied 2nd	Semifinals	8th UPI	NIT 1st Round
1974-75	23-8	.742	8-4	Tied 2nd	Champion	9th AP, 10th UPI	NCAA Final 16
1975-76	25-4	.862	11-1	First	Finalist	8th AP, 6th UPI	NCAA 1st Round
1976-77	28-5	.848	9-3	First	Champion	5th AP, 3rd UPI	NCAA Runner-up
1977-78	23-8	.742	9-3	First	Semifinals	10th UPI	NCAA 1st Round
1978-79	23-0	.793	9-0	Tied 1st	Champion	9th AP, 3rd UPI	NCAA 2nd Round
1979-80	21-8	.724	9-5	Tied 2nd	Semifinals	15th AP & UPI	NCAA 2nd Round
1980-81	29-8	.784	10-4	Second	Champion	6th AP & UPI	NCAA Runner-up
1981-82	32-2	.941	12-2	Tied 1st	Champion	1st AP & UPI	NCAA Champion
1982-83	28-8	.778	12-2	Tied 1st	Semifinals	8th AP & UPI	NCAA Final 8
1983-84	28-3	.903	14-0	First	Semifinals	1st AP & UPI	NCAA Final 16
1984-85	27-9	.750	9-5	Tied 1st	Finalist	7th AP & UPI	NCAA Final 8
1985-86	28-6	.824	10-4	Third	Quarterfinals	8th AP & UPI	NCAA Final 16
1986-87	32-4	.889	14-0	First	Finalist	2nd AP, 3rd UPI	NCAA Final 8
1987-88	27-7	.794	11-3	First	Finalist	7th AP, 8th UPI	NCAA Final 8
1988-89	29-8	.784	9-5	Tied 2nd	Champion	5th AP, 4th UPI	NCAA Final 16
1989-90	21-13	.618	8-6	Tied 3rd	Quarterfinals		NCAA Final 16
Totals 29 Years	688-203	.772	287-103 (.736)	15 ACC Regular-Season Titles	10 ACC Tournament Champion-ships / 15 ACC Tournament Finals	19 Top-10 Poll Finishes / 22 Top-20 Poll Finishes	20 NCAA's / 4 NIT's / 1 NCAA Title / 7 NCAA Regional Titles / 1 NIT Title

victories at that rate for a period of 21 years. Smith's career winning percentage of .773 is equally amazing, especially considering that his UNC teams seldom schedule cream-puff opposition. Reaching the NCAA Tournament field is the goal of every Division I school, but it's a normal procedure for Carolina under Smith, who has taken his team to the big event 16 successive years. In addition to the 1982 national title, his Tar Heels have reached the Final Four six times and were NCAA runners-up three of those six years.

The numbers affirm that Smith is one of the giants of his profession. But statistics reveal only part of the story. What was behind his ascension to the pinnacle of college coaching, and what has kept him there?

Dick Harp, a former head coach at Kansas University who had the opportunity to both coach Smith the player and work with Smith the coach, provided one answer. Harp was an assistant to Dr. F. C. "Phog" Allen, the head coach at Kansas when Smith played there and a man recognized as a major influence on the game. Harp also served on Smith's North Carolina staff as an administrative assistant for three years before retiring. "I really think Dean has had a significant impact on the game of basketball," said Harp. "Dean has done some tremendous things in basketball. The most obvious is his end-of-the-game stuff—saving his time-outs. Another is the acknowledgment of a good pass his North Carolina players make [the recipient pointing to the passer in acknowledgment]. This was referred to as Mickey Mouse stuff for a while, but now even the pros do it. In many ways, Dean has been ahead of his time. I don't think there is any question about his national impact. No question."

Harp also talked about the rich tradition Smith has built, based on a foundation of players who possess not only outstanding athletic ability, but attributes that help represent UNC well off the court, too. "Dean has continued to have outstanding teams with excellent character, and they are a joy to watch play," Harp said. "The players have so much enthusiasm for the game and for each other, and Dean puts teams like this on the floor year after year. I think that makes him a superb coach. He has a prestige-type program going for him now, and that helps in recruiting. Recruiting is big-business-like and highly pressurized. One thing I know, though, and that is Dean will remain ethical. Because of the kind of program he has developed and the kind of man he is, Dean is awfully hard to recruit against. And he is highly respected everywhere by those in basketball and those who know the game."

As construction neared completion and the dream that North Carolina would soon be playing basketball in a shiny new showplace became a reality, UNC alumni and the ACC athletic community buzzed with talk that the facility would be named for Smith.

Not surprising—to those who know him—was Smith's disapproval of such an idea. He was embarrassed at the thought of coaching in a place named for him. Smith would have liked all of his players to be honored. "They are the reason it has been built," he said.

He was fighting a losing battle. It was implausible to think that the Tar Heels' glossy basketball playground could be named for anyone other than Dean Edwards Smith. There was no one—other than Smith himself—who disagreed. The overwhelming support his name received from the UNC academic community demonstrated just how highly the coach is thought of as a member of the university.

Dr. Christopher Fordham was UNC's chancellor at the time a name was being considered for the new arena. He recalled the process as a "no-question" situation. "Recommendations came from all over the place to the chancellor," Fordham said. "I took them to the faculty committee, and that committee made its recommendations. I took them to the trustees. The main criteria in choosing a name for the student activities center went largely unspoken. It was character. The man [Smith] has a depth of character that enriches and ennobles the university."

Fordham noted that during the process of naming the basketball complex, he talked with the Tar Heels' coach. "I asked him about naming it for him and received his permission," Fordham said. "His reaction was one of typical modesty, almost reluctance, but he was gracious. Dean knew the university meant business about this matter, so he went ahead and agreed to it. Actually, I didn't give him very much of an opportunity to decline. I told him that's what the university wanted to do. He was his usual modest self—the reaction you'd expect from him. I know it was the one I expected, because I have known Dean a long time. We had been friends before then."

The former chancellor said Smith's image is so good and so solid that many people are tempted to discount it. "I guess that's human nature," Fordham said. "But let me tell you, Dean Smith's image is real—even if it seems too good to be true. Oh, he'll be the first to tell you he's not perfect, that he's far from it. That isn't the point, though; Dean strives to be a good person and do things the right way. That's why he has been such a wonderful ambassador for the University of North Carolina. He's a very good citizen of the university.

"Dean has always fostered an interest in public schools and in education. He also does a lot of community-service things, but has remained low-key about them. Like most people with a big heart, he's not looking for people to know about the things he does. As a coach, he doesn't think the focus ought to be on him, so he directs it to his players. Dean is modest, but it's not a false modesty. That's just a common thread, his normal way of living and functioning."

Fordham called Smith "an available resource" for UNC. "He's been that for athletics in our university and throughout the nation, especially in terms of the well-being of athletes. He has advised the chancellor on many things, among them athletic policy."

So it was that on Friday, January 17, 1986, at a black-tie affair, UNC's new roundball complex was officially named the Dean E. Smith Student Activities Center. In making the announcement, Fordham said, "Dean Smith is a molder of true student-athletes. He has a long history of developing student-athletes who excel in collegiate athletics, but who also become doctors, lawyers, coaches, teachers, and businessmen. He has shown us and the nation that intercollegiate sports and the academic nurturing of young athletes can be successfully combined."

The occasion that night was not only the dedication of a brand-new home for Tar Heel basketball, but the raising of money for the university's College of Arts and Sciences as well. Smith pointed this out, emphasizing that those paying to attend the ceremony were contributing money for academics, not the basketball arena, which had already been paid for.

What almost $34 million bought is one of the nation's largest and most prestigious coliseums, and a lasting tribute to one of college basketball's finest-ever coaches. It seats 21,444, has an area of 300,000 square feet, and measures 14 stories from its floor to the peak of its skylighted roof. The building is octagonal in shape and tan in color, blending nicely with the natural landscape. It is tucked comfortably in a wooded area.

The Smith Center's second level includes the athletic, basketball, sports information, and ticket offices. There are parquet floors. Twelve-foot-high glass doors open into the UNC Memorabilia Room, a miniature museum that holds artifacts and highlight tapes of some of the greatest moments in Carolina athletic history. The first level contains the best in training facilities. The amenities include a basketball locker room and lounge, as well as two swimming-team locker rooms. There are also a state-of-the-art training room and a weightroom.

The arena has a roomy concourse, lighted naturally through tinted glass. The lower level has 9,000 seats, with nearly 12,500 in the upper level. All are chair seats that face midcourt, and none is more than 150 feet from the arena floor. That floor is one of the few in the nation that has springs underneath. Layered with wooden beams and plywood and covered by the maple floor, the springs produce a resilience

The house that Dean built

that helps reduce ankle and knee injuries. Four scoreboards allow all fans to see the score without a turn of the head. Electronic message centers flash words and pictures in a variety of colors. Brought from Carmichael and added to all the modern frills were the symbols of a powerful past—the banners signifying conference, tournament, and national championships hang in the rafters. Their number seems to increase almost yearly.

Majestic is the word used in the Carolina basketball media guide to describe the Smith Center. A more appropriate adjective is difficult to think of, especially for people walking into the complex at times when no game or concert is being held. Its expanse swallows a visitor.

As those on hand toured the facility on dedication night, Smith spoke about the honor of having the building named for him. Rather, he tried to shy away from talk of it. "It has never been a goal of mine," he said. "I never wanted a building or a street named for me. I just hope in the new building we maintain our good sportsmanship. No profanity. No arm waving on free throws. And I hope we'll continue applauding other teams' players when they're introduced as our guests."

Many of the conversations that evening involved what was to be the real christening of the complex. Archrival Duke's basketball team was paying a visit the next day. How perfect. North Carolina was ranked number one in the national polls, with Duke in the third spot. Both were unbeaten, the Tar Heels at 17–0 and the Blue Devils at 16–0. Sentiment said UNC should win, but the opposition promised it would be mighty tough.

Asked if the game was special to him because it was to be his first in a new arena bearing his name, Smith was typically unmoved by such emotions connected to an athletic contest. "What if we lose?" someone asked. Smith repeated the question, then answered, "Well, I'd get up Sunday morning, and I'd be all right. I call this kind of game fun—but because of the teams and how well they have been playing. I certainly don't feel any pressure to win this game because it is the first in this place. And our players shouldn't."

The game was a classic, and regardless of whether the fact that they were baptizing a new coliseum had anything to do with it, the Tar Heels performed as if they were on a mission. NBA star-to-be Brad Daugherty scored 23 points and grabbed 11 rebounds, with Steve Hale pouring in 28 points. The final score was North Carolina 95, Duke 92. A sign that emerged from the sea of Carolina fans during the game told a lot about feelings for the new building. "The Tradition Continues," it read.

It wasn't long thereafter that the Smith Center started to be called the Dean Dome, and that is how the place is referred to most often. Bill Cosby, Bruce Springsteen, and many others have performed in the imposing complex, but as UNC Athletic Director John Swofford said at the opening, "It is first and foremost a basketball facility. It is certainly multipurpose, but it was built mainly because of a successful basketball program over the past few years."

Few years was a decided understatement. The consistency of the Tar Heel program under the direction of Smith has proven one thing: that those charged with naming the University of North Carolina's student activities center were right on target.

After all, the place really is the house that Dean built.

LOOKING BACK

Dean Smith never had a definite plan to be a basketball coach; he never made any announcement to that effect. It just sort of happened, perhaps because his father was a coach. More importantly, though, Smith was always coaching in his own mind, trying even as a young boy to figure the strategies of sports. He grew up analyzing the hows and whys of particular games, and by the time he was a senior at Kansas University, he was an unofficial aide to one of the greatest coaches ever.

Alfred and Vesta Smith are both Kansas natives. Alfred coached at Emporia High School—13 years of basketball, 12 of football, six of track, and one of baseball. Later, upon moving to Topeka, he accepted a position as recreation director at the veterans hospital. Mrs. Smith taught high school before teaching child development and child psychology at Kansas State

Vesta and Alfred Smith in 1982

Photo by Hugh Morton

Teachers College in Emporia. She also served as superinten-
dent of the Lyon County schools while the family was living
in Emporia. Her given name, Vesta, refers to the goddess of
the hearth and home in Roman mythology; Mrs. Smith took
great pride in being a good mother and homemaker, inter-
rupting her teaching career to remain home with her children
until they reached junior-high age.

Two children were born to Alfred and Vesta Smith. The
elder was a daughter named Joan, gifted in music and in the
classroom. Her academic achievements eventually earned her
a Bachelor of Science degree in education from Kansas State
Teachers College. She then won fellowships to the University

of Chicago, where she received a master's degree with a double major in religion and education. The son, Dean, two and a half years younger than his sister, was born February 28, 1931. As a youngster, his interests were varied and included music, but his first love was athletics of any kind. His strongest classroom subject was math.

In the mid-1930s, Emporia had a population of approximately 12,000. The Smith family lived in a moderately simple one-and-a-half-story stucco house at 1217 Washington Street. The neighborhood was comfortably situated a few blocks from the downtown area and was inhabited primarily by professors at Kansas State Teachers College and their families. In the Smiths' driveway was a Ford automobile, first a 1929 model purchased after Alfred and Vesta's marriage, then a 1935 model. The family pet was a dog named Micky, a mixed breed. Apparently let out of the wagon of a passing farmer, she was picked up by four-year-old Dean and became part of the family for 11 years until she died shortly before the move to Topeka.

The Smiths used a simple formula for raising their children. "Love and discipline will go a long way," Mr. Smith recalled, "and they worked pretty well for us. Mrs. Smith demanded the same discipline at home that she got in the classroom; she was quite strict. I was away a lot because of coaching. . . . Mrs. Smith deserves much of the credit because she had a great deal to do with the children and their growing up." The Smiths were actively involved in church life and were strong Baptists. "We raised the children up in the church," Mr. Smith said. "Sometimes there was some kidding about Dean going to church four times every Sunday; but really, it was Sunday school and preaching in the morning, then youth work and preaching again in the evening. I think he always enjoyed the church youth program and stayed very active in it."

Today, Dean Smith is applauded for his innovative mind. His mother recalls his curiosity as a small boy. "I used to call

The young Dean Smith with his father

him Christopher Pete," she said. "The Christopher was for the explorer Christopher Columbus. . . . Dean was forever investigating everything like a little detective. When he was real little, about two or three, all of us would laugh and say, 'Well, Dean will be around to see about that,' because whatever it was, he would be checking on things. Even before he could talk, he was looking into everything and analyzing whatever he could."

Much of Mrs. Smith's leisure time was spent attending games coached by her husband. Dean kept close tabs on sports even then and was able to tell anyone who asked which Emporia High player wore a certain number. "I carried 25 players on the football team," Mr. Smith remembered. "When we went to eat as a team and sat around the table, some of the boys would have some fun with Dean. They'd pick a number out of the 25 our players wore on their jerseys and would ask Dean something like, 'Now, who is number 99?' He'd say right away who wore that number, and we all got a kick out of that. Dean was only four or five at the time."

He loved spending time with his father and the teams, but he was interested in other things, too. "Dean was just . . . a very average boy," Mrs. Smith said. "He and his sister were always happy children; and Mr. Smith and I were sure glad for that. Dean had a bicycle and played with the neighborhood children. . . . I hired a teacher to give Dean piano lessons. I could play but thought it better for someone outside the family to teach my son. I helped Dean with practice, and he learned to read music. But after about three years, when he was in the fourth grade, he began to take more interest in sports. He never did have much time to practice anymore, so I quit paying for the lessons."

"I have good childhood memories," Dean Smith reflected. "It was normal Middle American, I'd say. There were always sports. There was this vacant lot two doors away from us. It's no longer vacant, but back then a group of us boys always played baseball and football there. I used to catch Dick Hiskey, now the head of the Chemistry Department at the University of North Carolina, and he was an excellent pitcher. One day, I got hit by a foul tip in the throat and said that would be the last time I would catch without a mask. A couple of buddies and I sometimes even sold Cokes at that lot, I think for five cents each."

Dean participated in basketball, football, and baseball youth leagues in season. He also became quite skillful at table tennis. Thanks to constant practice on his family's Ping-Pong table, he became the state table-tennis champion in the 13-year-old age group. It was while playing Ping-Pong with his father that Dean learned a valuable lesson, one he would later teach to his players at the University of North Carolina on the basketball floor. The lesson, subtly taught, was explained by Mr. Smith. "When Dean was still real young, about nine or 10 years old," he said, "I played him every day in Ping-Pong. I'd get on up to 19 points, but I'd let him come on back and win, so he would learn to win in the pinch. Pretty soon he did it on his own, but I was trying to encourage him to make a come-back and never quit. I'd let him come back and win something like 21 to 19 and hoped this would give him courage and confidence that he could come from behind. Of course, I beat him pretty soundly sometimes, too, to teach him what losing was. That was part of the game."

If Dean acquired his interest in athletics and coaching from his father, it is likely he gained his propensity for organization and detail from his mother. "He's a detail man," Mr. Smith said of his son, "and that's the way his mother is. I'm a little careless, and might leave my clothes lying around someplace, but not Mrs. Smith and not Dean. She always kept everything where it should be, and Dean was the same way with his things as far back as I can remember."

"My family always saw things through and worked hard," Mrs. Smith said. "We didn't believe in shortcuts, and Dean never tried any either. He participated in all sports and real-ized how difficult playing is, and I think this helped him after he became a coach. But he worked very hard. If he lost, he wasn't the kind to give up; neither was his dad. They worked at whatever it was, trying to find new avenues. They found them, too."

"Being the high school coach, Dad had the key to the gym, and I'd get to go there to play sometimes," Smith recalled. "I enjoyed being the son of the local high school coach. I started playing sports very early, but I was about the best athlete I would ever become in the ninth grade. I didn't improve much after that. I was five-ten in height then and thought I'd grow to be about six-four. But I didn't grow any more at all. I can even remember asking Dick Harp at Kansas if I could be listed on our official roster as five-eleven. I was the shortest player on the squad. I think I probably liked football better than the other sports when I was in junior high and high school. That was mainly because I was the quarterback. People thought more of football than other sports where I was growing up, and we once had 13,000 to 14,000 people [in Lawrence Stadium, which had a capacity of 10,000] for a high school game in Wichita."

As head basketball coach at the University of North Carolina, Smith has been known to divulge information about his team's tactics to interested fellow coaches, and he has always been eager to share basketball concepts. "Dean is not a bit selfish," Mrs. Smith said. "I remember once when we had just given him his first allowance. He and his sister each got a quarter, and that was in the days when a quarter was worth 25 cents. Well, I took all this time explaining how Dean could give part of the money to Sunday school and keep some out to save. So he understood very well. The boys who were his friends gathered around about that time, and all of them hopped on their bicycles to go down to a little grocery store near our house. It wasn't very long until they were back, but Dean's money was all gone. I said, 'Dean, you only get the quarter this one time, and then you have to wait until next week.' Then his dad came home, and Dean told him the whole thing. So Dad gave him another quarter, and that solved the problem; but it didn't teach Dean anything."

"My folks always felt there were more important things than money," Smith said. "Mom was more of the saver, and I guess I was more like Dad with money. Mine was always spent. I was taught values, though, first of all through the church. The youth group was important; I think there was one year we even had youth meetings every day after school. We didn't have the academic pressure some youngsters have

The Smith family around the time Joan graduated from junior
high and Dean from grammar school

today, but I remember that my dad was very good at making my sister and me competitive. She had gone through junior high and made only two B's, the rest A's, so Dad told me if I could match that, he would give me a hundred dollars. I matched it. But I wasn't pushed to study."

One of the saddest moments of Dean's life came when he was in junior high school. His reaction to tragedy told much about his character. Dean had a close friend named Shad Woodruff. Shad was short for Shadow, a nickname derived from the fact that Dean's friend imitated everything his older brother did. Shad and Dean were teammates on a junior high squad that was enjoying great success. Then, one day, Shad was taken to the hospital. His illness was diagnosed as polio, and it was an anxious Smith family that worried and wondered, since Dean and Shad had drunk from the same soft-drink bottle only a few days earlier.

"We didn't know if Dean had been exposed," Mrs. Smith said, "but he was all right. He couldn't enter Shad's room, so he stood outside the door. Within the day, Shad was taken, and that was a terrible loss. Dean had a good idea, though. I had cut all the little articles about the junior high team out of the paper, so Dean took them and made them into a scrapbook to give to Shad's mother. He did that on his own."

Dean's sister, Joan, saw in the incident a hint of the strength that would distinguish her brother's personality. "I was very impressed with Dean's own personal attitude when Shad died," she said. "I was around the house crying and feeling like the world had caved in, and our folks were upset. Dean never shed a tear that we were aware of; he was quiet and just sat out on the front porch and cut out all his pictures to make that scrapbook. That was his tribute to Shad; and in his own quiet way, this was how he handled his grief.

"To me, this was symbolic of the kind of person Dean is today. He never moped and never felt sorry for himself. He is still the same way, taking whatever is at hand that he has to deal with and making the best of it. Dean never looks for any excuse and never looks for anyone to blame. 'That's the way it was; I did my best' is the way he accepts whatever has happened. Then he picks up from there and deals with the situation by doing something positive about it."

Another characteristic of Dean Smith the coach that remains from Dean Smith the boy is the ability to accept defeat. An extremely competitive man, he maintains a calm, collected disposition on the outside even though he may be churning inside. "Dean was very competitive and still is," Mrs. Smith reflected, "but he kept his disappointment inside. He didn't like losing, but he just usually looked forward to the next time. He didn't stomp or pout or anything like that."

"He was better at losing than his mother and me," Mr. Smith remembered. "We're poor losers. We still get upset if North Carolina loses. Dean doesn't like to lose, I'll tell you that for sure. It's inside him more; he doesn't let it show. I can't recall him scowling or doing anything like that. I think Dean took it more or less in stride, but I know he was suffering inside when he lost. There never was any temper, though, and I'll tell you something else—Dean never cursed. I've never heard him utter one curse word."

Joan pointed out how her brother simply accepts what is, rather than offers alibis or upsets himself with what might have been. "He has never been one to wish that things were different," she said. "Dean just works with what is there, and I have always thought that to be a genius of his personality. He has always been in control, but it isn't the kind of control that is stuffy. And he isn't goody-goody. People always knew they could count on Dean, and they still can. He has kept things in such good perspective; that's why he can take losses, that's why he can take disappointments, that's why he can take grief and sadness. He's had all these things in his life—you can't live as long as he has and not have some problems. In the long run, though, Dean knows what's really important is his own impression of himself, his own integrity, and the ability to look himself in the mirror every morning and know he doesn't have to be ashamed of himself."

As Dean grew, so did his interest in dissecting athletic contests and trying to decide how strategies could have worked better. Both the games he played and the ones his father coached were torn apart in the Smith living room. "I won't say I asked him to help me coach," Mr. Smith said, "but I won't say I turned down his suggestions either." Plays and strategy were discussed and diagnosed. Dean Smith was becoming a coach.

"I don't know how much of it he really got from me," Mr. Smith said. "I was an ordinary coach. I once had a basketball team to win the state championship. Dean just grew up with coaching and was interested in it. I would say after a while that it became more or less understood coaching is what he wanted to do. He just grew into it. But he always had an eye and a mind for the job."

Dean played the thinking man's positions: quarterback in football, point guard in basketball, and catcher in baseball. Calling plays and pitches helped enable him to think like a coach.

He was often the captain of his junior high teams. And sometimes his confidence flowed a bit too abundantly. "There were times he could be an obnoxious little brother," Joan remembered. "I'm not saying in junior high that he didn't think he was the coolest customer in eighth or ninth grade, but fortunately, he had this other side to him which couldn't stand a person who was cocky."

"I was very cocky in the eighth grade," Smith said. "Joan gave me a talk and helped me understand that I didn't know it all and that the world didn't revolve around me. As a result, I think I went the other route for a while, being overly modest about taking a compliment. My sister and I had a great relationship after my eighth-grade year, after the usual things brothers and sisters go through. It was really nice to have someone to talk to, someone who was close to being the same age as I was."

After Dean's freshman year in Emporia came the move to Topeka, where he attended Topeka High. The change in scen-

Dean Smith in 1949

ery made little difference. Dean was still well liked. He immediately became a starter in three sports, just as he had been at Emporia High. His senior season, he called every offensive play in football, and his team finished second in the state. In basketball, Dean and his teammates came close to a championship his junior season, only to be handed a disappointing loss in the state semifinals. His senior year, Topeka High was beaten by the Wichita East team of Ralph Miller (who retired as Oregon State coach after the 1989 season) in the state tournament. Smith and his teammates did win a state baseball championship over an excellent Wichita North team.

The Smith family remained close throughout Dean's high school days and attended as many of his games as possible. "Sports were kind of a social thing with our family," Smith recalled. "My whole family enjoyed going to watch my games. My folks possibly put too much emphasis on athletics, although they never pressured me. It was just that there were no other things to do. I enjoyed sports and was fortunate enough to play pretty well, well enough to be picked early when we chose sides."

Dean was considering a career in medicine and was prodded by a Topeka businessman to major in premed at Columbia University in New York. A Topeka physician suggested a career in optometry. Other local businessmen promised opportunities after college. Dean's strong math background suggested another possible field of study. He did not make his choice until much later, leaving himself open to several options.

Kansas State Assistant Coach Tex Winter offered Dean a tempting partial grant-in-aid for basketball. Smith was not highly recruited, though. He finally chose to attend Kansas University partly for sentimental reasons, since his father had gone there for his master's degree. His tremendous respect for Kansas's basketball coach, Dr. F. C. "Phog" Allen, also propelled him toward the Jayhawks. Outstanding high school grades helped him earn an academic grant, and Allen helped him get a job selling programs at varsity football games to make spending money as a freshman.

Dean played both football and basketball his first year, but then gave up football on the advice of his father, who said, "I thought Dean's best sport was basketball; and besides, he only weighed 155 pounds when he was a freshman." Dean also lettered in baseball, playing catcher. Eventually, he was awarded an athletic scholarship in addition to his scholastic grant.

"Looking back, I was very mediocre at all three sports," Smith recalled. "I quit baseball my senior year for two reasons. I was late coming out for the team because of basketball, and by that time, Galen Fiss [who later played professional football with the Cleveland Browns] had beaten me out. He was always a better player, but he finally learned how to handle pitchers."

It was an educational experience playing basketball for Dr. Allen, considered one of the most creative and successful college basketball coaches of all time and recognized today as the father of basketball coaching. Allen died in 1974 at the age of 88 after establishing numerous trends in college basketball. In 39 years of coaching the Jayhawks, he amassed 590 wins, second only to one of his star pupils, Kentucky's legendary Adolph Rupp, in total NCAA victories at the time of his death. Allen was to have a tremendous influence on another star pupil, Dean Smith.

"Phog Allen was so much on a pedestal," Smith said. "I remember I tried to call him Dr. Allen, but he told me, 'Just call me Doc.' Doc Allen was a great psychologist. He could give some kind of pep talks. We thought some were very funny and we'd laugh, then he'd have us in tears with others."

As an assistant to Allen, Dick Harp was highly respected by the Jayhawk players. He later became Kansas's head coach for eight years; ironically, it was in his initial season, 1956–57, that the Jayhawks lost to North Carolina for the national

Dr. F. C. "Phog" Allen

Dick Harp

championship, 54–53 in triple overtime. "He had the brightest basketball mind of anyone I've ever known," Smith said of Harp.

Dick Harp came to know Smith quite well from the time Dean assisted him with the Kansas freshman team. Smith was the top guard reserve for the varsity as the Jayhawks won the NCAA championship in 1952, his junior year, although his 1.6 scoring average that season did not reflect his total contribution. Kansas reached the finals the next season, only to finish runner-up. Smith was aggressive, smart, and scrappy when he got his chance to play. He was also talented, but he was stuck in the shadow of other exceptional guards. Harp's description of Smith the player brings to mind some of the words used today to characterize Smith the coach. "He was a skillful player, as he is a skillful coach," Harp said, "and he was a creative player, just as he is a creative coach. Dean was bright and alert, and he was interested in learning about basketball. I have fond memories of working with Dean in running the red-shirt team's offense."

Smith remembers thinking that his informal coaching assignment might cut down on his playing time. "But it didn't," he said. "I might be the first or the last substitute, but I certainly wasn't put in to score [he totaled 80 points for his collegiate career]. I went in to lead the team. But Dad had always said you don't go by points in judging what a player contributes. That's what the coaches liked—that I didn't look for the shot. My senior year, our coaches were nice to say our team had six starters, but I only started a couple of times. I may have gone somewhere else and played more, but it obviously was better to be a reserve on a team which finished second or first nationally."

Smith accepted his role as backup guard but retained confidence in his ability. "Kansas University was playing Kansas State in Manhattan, Kansas," Dean's father recalled. "Dean went up for a rebound, someone went over his back, and a foul was called. On the way to the other end of the court to shoot the free throw, Dean's teammate Dean Kelley came up and put his arm around my son. Everyone thought Kelley was encouraging Dean, and after the game, a reporter asked what Kelley had said. 'Nothing,' Dean said. 'I just bet him a Coke I'd make the free throw.' Well, he did, and Kansas won the game."

Anyone familiar with Tar Heel basketball knows Smith's players work very hard at getting defensive position and drawing charging fouls. Every time Harp sees it happen, he smiles to himself. "Yes," he said, "when I see that, I think of Dean taking a charge once and very nearly breaking his thumb. He played basketball very much like he coaches it. Dean was handicapped at the time he played because one of our starting guards was much taller and the other was all-conference. Our players at that time were really outstanding, and Dean might have played much more somewhere else. We didn't substitute as frequently then as Dean does, so reserves didn't get in all that often."

Smith's interest in coaching continued to grow in college. "It was obvious that the interest was there," Harp recalled. "His dad had been a coach, and there was no question he was an analytical young man, so I don't find it hard to understand his success. He was a bright person to begin with, was creative, and gave every evidence then of having the kind of grasp on basketball which he has now. He was a very understanding player and always knew what he was supposed to be doing."

Smith took full advantage of Phog Allen's wisdom and experience, which offered a rare opportunity for someone eager to learn more about basketball. "There are two things about Dr. Allen which I feel Dean absorbed and which I feel have helped him a great deal," Harp noted. "First and foremost, Doc was a fundamentalist. He believed if an athlete couldn't perform the fundamentals, he couldn't play. Doc was always hard-put for the kid who had one skill—like shooting, for example—but couldn't do anything else. That bothered him. I think . . . he was by far the most significant developer of fundamental ideas about the game in its history. Secondly, Doc was an inspirational coach. I would say in both instances Dean is a lot like Doc was; those two things, along with players, make great teams.

"Doc was much broader than the game of basketball," Harp said. "He knew there was a great deal more to life than playing basketball. He was a very charismatic coach. Dean is much the same."

The player-coach relationship Smith and Harp enjoyed was a close one, and the two remain fast friends today. "The man has changed very little," Harp said of Smith, "and this is a credit to him. He has stayed on an even keel without being swayed by his fame or popularity. Dean is very modest, despite having accomplished so much. There is no way to look back and not be surprised at the impact he has had on the game. It wasn't possible to project that he would have the kind of rapport and understanding of young people and that he would establish the kind of standards that would attract great basketball players who are also fine young men. That's the thing he has put with his other attributes to make his program a success. Dean was always thinking as a player. Even on the bench he would figure what should be done in certain situations. I guess he's always been at it."

One of the guards Smith played behind at Kansas was Gil Reich, a fraternity brother of Dean's at Phi Gamma Delta and an all-American football player. Now an executive vice-president for Equitable Life Assurance Society of America, Reich remembers Smith as an unofficial player-coach even in college. "Dean was very religious and came from a very devout family," Reich said, "and many of us thought maybe he would become a minister. But it became kind of understood, an unspoken thing, that he would go into coaching. Dean never talked about it, though; it was just implied. He was accepted by the rest of us players as a sort of player-assistant, and I remember him working with Coach Allen and Coach

Harp. In fact, Dean helped Coach Allen quite a bit in developing our half-court pressure defense, and it was a key to our national championship in 1952."

Reich noticed Dean's talent as a recruiter even in college. "We'd try to recruit guys to join our fraternity," Reich said. "Dean showed an ability to do it well. He was a salesman, I guess you'd say; anyway, he could get along with all kinds of people. That's why he has recruited so well as a coach. He goes after a certain type of player, really a certain type of young man. The type of guy Dean is comes across through his players. I met Phil Ford and could see some of Dean in him. His players seem to be a cut above the average athlete. Undoubtedly, Dean's relationship with his players is the key. I must say that I am not at all surprised at anything Dean Smith has done, not after knowing him."

Many of Smith's most enjoyable college experiences resulted from close friendships he built in Phi Gamma Delta, even though, as he said, "I'm not what you'd really call a fraternity man." After placing 37th out of 647 in his high school graduating class, Smith completed his four years at Kansas with "about a B-minus average, I'd guess. I didn't work as hard academically as I should have. I made A's in some things, but the only D that I remember was in speech. I guess that's the reason I still hate to make speeches."

While Smith was in college, he and all the other Kansas athletes joined Air Force ROTC, mainly to avoid being drafted. "I knew I had my stint to do," Smith said, "but during my senior year at Kansas, I didn't worry about the future."

Upon graduation, a number of possible vocations awaited Smith, but so did a hitch of military duty. An overseas tour was ahead, along with the official beginning of one of the most acclaimed coaching careers in the history of college basketball.

THE EARLY YEARS

In 1961, upon announcing his resignation as the University of North Carolina head basketball coach, Frank McGuire made a prediction. It concerned the future of his successor, the practically unknown Dean Smith. "Dean Smith will be one of the finest coaches in the nation within a very few years," McGuire said.

Though that bit of prognosticating would prove more accurate than even McGuire could have anticipated, the picture took quite awhile unfolding. Just as is the case in almost every endeavor, greatness was not achieved overnight. Strapped by an NCAA probation he inherited, Smith was to experience a losing season as a rookie coach and a 12–12 season in which, by his own admission, he did the worst job of his career. He was also to suffer the pain of seeing himself hung in effigy by students on the North Carolina campus. His start as the coach of one of the most successful athletic programs in collegiate history was inauspicious, to say the least.

In 1953, Kansas University's graduating class included Dean Smith, who figured he would eventually accept a high school coaching offer somewhere in his home state.

While waiting for his military call, Smith assisted Dr. F. C. "Phog" Allen and Dick Harp with the Kansas basketball team. He obtained a job in Lawrence, Kansas, doing clerical work with a paper company and played semipro basketball in Parsons, Kansas—a town that would later send him his chief assistant at North Carolina. Smith helped with the Jayhawk team from October until the Big Eight Tournament. At that time, in February 1954, the Air Force beckoned, and Smith entered as a second lieutenant.

He was sent to Texas for processing, then to Scott Air Force Base just outside St. Louis, where he attended electronics school. There, Smith played volleyball and baseball. Finally, he was stationed in Furstenfeldbruck, Germany, near Munich, a tour that would last a year and two months.

In 1955, during Smith's German assignment, he played basketball. That fall, he also began to coach. "I'll always remember that team," Smith said. "We were undefeated, 11–0, while I was coaching. We had seven air policemen, and one of the guys was six-foot-seven. I played myself all the time—everyone always gets better after they get out of college, you know. . . . All the members of that team really wanted to play, which made coaching easy; and it was great fun. That experience just whetted my appetite to coach. Those guys got together and gave me a watch, one I still wear occasionally, along with those I have received in NCAA Tournaments."

By then, Smith had a good idea where his career was headed. "I remember my sophomore year in college, Doc Allen told me to plan for medical school. 'There are too many ups and downs in coaching,' he said. I can't recall exactly when, but I decided, heck, I might as well coach. I do remember kind of always thinking I'd become a coach, though."

While in Germany, Smith met Bob Spear, who became a lifelong friend as well as a link to a college coaching oppor-

Bob Spear

tunity, thus eliminating a start on the high school level. Spear was coaching an Air Force team from France at the time. Their teams met, and the two made an acquaintance as a result.

"Dean and I spent some real good evenings discussing the various phases of basketball," Spear recalled, "and I got the impression quite readily and quite emphatically that he had a future in basketball. He had a lot of talent, not only as a player, but more specifically as a basketball mind and coach. He was not a coach at that time, but was a player. I think he was helping with the coaching quite a lot, and it was actually through his Furstenfeldbruck coach, Jack Schwall, that I got to know Dean. Our paths just crossed, and it was the greatest thing ever to happen to me as far as my coaching career was concerned."

It was not long thereafter that the United States Air Force Academy was established in Denver. (It would move to its permanent home in Colorado Springs in August 1958.) Spear, who had been an assistant coach at the Naval Academy, was named the first Air Force Academy head basketball coach. "When that selection was made," Spear said, "the first one I could think of to be my assistant was Dean Smith. So, naturally, I did everything I could through the military and the chain of command to get him out of Germany and back to Denver.

"Dean had an impressive personality from the start," Spear remembered. "I thought we'd make a good team because the initial Air Force basketball program would be strengthened by people with different points of view which would blend together. Dean was the logical choice, and for me, there wasn't going to be any other."

Smith recalled some of the complications involved. "I only had a two-year commitment to the Air Force," he said. "If I signed an indefinite [commitment], I would be in for three more years. I wanted to know I would get the coaching job at the Air Force Academy for sure. Finally, they told me if I would sign the indefinite, I would get the academy assignment. I was a first lieutenant by then and made captain upon being discharged."

Slicing through the red tape required three or four months, and it was December 1955 before Smith returned home from Germany. "I didn't report to the Air Force Academy until January of '56," Smith said. "That first season, we played freshman teams." Spear and Smith were off on their laborious, yet exciting, task of putting together a brand-new college basketball team. The college coaching career of Dean Smith was quietly under way.

Organizing and molding a collegiate basketball team is no easy project under any circumstances, but at a military academy, where there are so many limitations on the young men who can be recruited, the challenge can be monstrous. There were only about 300 cadets on the Air Force Academy campus in those days, and the college was experiencing growing pains. Nevertheless, Spear and Smith found the effort enriching. Smith's duties were not confined to basketball, as the infant academy was not large enough to provide a different coach for each sport. Smith coached the Falcon baseball team one spring. His very first head-coaching position on the collegiate level was directing the Air Force Academy golf team, one that finished with a 1–4–1 record. "I could tell how bad we were going to be right away," Smith said, "because I could beat some of the guys on the team."

Basketball was Smith's primary responsibility, however, and it became apparent to Spear quite early that his young assistant was on the way to making a name for himself in the game. "Dean's background and his knowledge of basketball along with my experience and ideas combined to make us a good coaching team," Spear said. "Things went together very well. It was easy to recognize the future Dean might have in basketball. His innovative thinking was obvious even in those early days of his coaching career. He was really the same Dean Smith everyone knows today."

Smith expressed mutual admiration for Spear, saying, "Bob

was a great teacher, a very patient man. Working with him at the Air Force Academy was a great learning experience. Bob had only one player recruited by other colleges, yet he beat some teams people wouldn't believe."

Spear recalled trying to decide on an offense for the Air Force Academy team. "Dean had quite a lot of experience in college with the shuffle offense which Bruce Drake had put in at the University of Oklahoma. Dean felt the shuffle would be ideal—a great offense for the type of material we had at the academy. It would allow us to move the ball and go for the good shot. We used it, and it did prove to be just the right thing for us."

Much has been said about Smith's ingenuity and his ability to communicate with his players. According to Spear, those characteristics were already surfacing in 1956. But the former Air Force Academy coach pointed to another of his assistant's assets as his strongest. "He was such a great teacher," Spear said, "and he still is. He could come up with new and exciting ideas, and then he could get them across so well to the players. The way he taught basketball and all its fundamentals was just another indication that Dean was to be extremely successful. That he could teach the way he could was probably the key to that success.

"Having ideas is wonderful, but you've got to make someone understand them," Spear said. "Dean did and still does. He was great to watch at practice. He was an ABC type of teacher and even started by saying, 'This is a basketball.' He would run through an individual drill and then carry it on to the two-man, three-man, four-man, and five-man concept until the drill was a complete team thing. He worked with the individual's position on the basketball court. He had everything totally organized, and he related to the players that they were there to learn and that there was a limited amount of time to accomplish the learning process. There was no fooling around; he made use of every minute, and the players' concentration was at the maximum level. Even with all of this,

Dean seemed to have a sixth sense. He was smart enough to perceive when stress and strain were setting in, and when that happened, he would back off. Practices with Dean in charge were really something to behold."

The Air Force Academy basketball team won 11 and lost 10 its first season, 1956–57, with a 17–6 record the next year. Both squads distinctly resembled today's North Carolina teams, though certainly not in talent. Smith's influence on the fledgling Falcons and Spear's influence on his assistant were jointly responsible for the similarities. Spear's Air Force Academy teams utilized the run-and-jump and point-zone defenses, while even showing a four-corners look on offense at times. All of those maneuvers were to become North Carolina trademarks. "We had a certain approach to four corners that was a little different," Spear said. "The way Dean runs it now is about the same as the spread offense which he designed for us. We spread people out all over the court with the idea of penetrating or driving to the basket, then either going all the way in or chipping off to the open man. Or we might rotate back around and take the ball back out front. However, we didn't have a Phil Ford to make things happen like Dean did. I'd say he first came up with that offense around 1958."

That year was to be Smith's last as an Air Force Academy assistant coach. The man he worked under saw clearly that his young aide was headed for an illustrious career. "I could see he had it all going for him," Spear said. "He knew and understood the game of basketball so well. He had new ideas, and he could teach. He had his players' dedication in listening to him and in executing for him. It's very rare for a coach to come along with all these qualities. He was a great planner, too, and did his homework. He always knew his opponents and their strengths and weaknesses. It was evident to me that he could do whatever he wanted—reach whatever goal he might have. Above all else about Dean, the thing I liked best then and still admire is his loyalty. He remembered every player and person with whom he worked, and this continues to be true. The players liked him, and Dean gained their respect because of his strong principles, stability, and the fact that he lives the life he teaches others to live.

"The kids also liked Dean because he never put pressure on them to win. I know for a fact that he still doesn't. He is a very competitive person. He likes to win, but he'll never criticize or blame a player for a loss. He won't pass the buck after a defeat."

Bob Spear wanted to see his good friend advance, but he had no idea just how rapidly Smith would move up the coaching ladder. Spear played the lead role in sending Smith off to Chapel Hill, where the Tar Heels and coaching fame were waiting.

Every year during the week of the NCAA basketball semifinals and finals, college coaches gather in the host city for their national convention. The year 1957 found hundreds of basketball coaches swarming in on Kansas City, Missouri. Most of the stories swapped during late-night sessions at such conventions remain behind closed doors, but occasionally an incident of note comes to public light. One such exchange occurred in 1957, the product of a meeting among old friends in a hotel room.

The group included Bob Spear and Naval Academy Coach Ben Carnevale, who had been the head coach at North Carolina in 1946–47. University of Denver Coach Hoyt Brawner and North Carolina Coach Frank McGuire were the other old friends. Their bond dated back many years, and each coaches' convention marked a renewal of acquaintances, as they held their own reunion. Joining them was Dean Smith, the five sharing a two-bedroom suite in the Continental Hotel. McGuire and Carnevale shared one room and Spear and Smith the other, while Brawner slept on the couch.

Smith clearly recalls the events that led to his becoming a University of North Carolina assistant coach. "We were having breakfast in our room the morning after the championship game," he said. "That's when Frank said, 'Buck [Freeman]

Smith with Frank McGuire

has been ill, and I may need an assistant next year or the following year.' Then Frank said, 'Ben and Bob tell me I should hire you, Dean.' I said, 'I don't know; whatever Bob says.'

"Well, we went away, and the next summer Frank came through Denver on the way to a coaching clinic. He called and said Buck was staying another year. Then he said, 'I hope it will work out next year.'

"So, in 1957–58, I stayed at the Air Force Academy. The next year, at the 1958 convention in Louisville, our same group stayed together again. The first night during dinner, Frank said, 'I hope you'll come and visit [Chapel Hill] and see if you like it.' On April 14, my family and I went on a weekend and looked at houses. I went back in May and bought a house. In August, we moved to Chapel Hill."

Smith also remembers his first meeting with Tar Heel players, which took place in 1957 after UNC won the national title. "Frank had the players up to our suite and asked if I'd say something," Smith said. "I chose Joe Quigg because he had made those big foul shots, and I said something about that. But I wasn't too happy. Remember, I knew all of the Kansas players well and, of course, had been pulling for them. Then Frank asked me to find a place to take the writers. My favorite place was Eddy's, kind of a nightclub which served very good food, but which was a bit expensive. I joked that I found the most expensive place I could, since North Carolina was paying the bill. This was around midnight. Eddy's stayed open, and we were there two or three hours."

Though Smith took a pay cut from what he had been earning as an officer and assistant coach at the Air Force Academy, he didn't leave for UNC because there were no other opportunities. Dick Harp had asked that his former player join him as the second assistant at Kansas.

As willing as he was, Smith contributed very little to the North Carolina basketball program at first. McGuire wanted his new assistant to become settled, to learn about the team, and to know the man with whom he was working. The Irishman had a lock on New York, as his strong contacts had created a virtual pipeline that sent high school basketball talent to Chapel Hill in droves. So there wasn't much recruiting to be done. And anyway, the North Carolina basketball house was in good order, the Tar Heels having captured the national championship with a perfect 32–0 record just the previous year. They then went 19–7 in 1957–58.

"I didn't know one soul in North Carolina," Smith said in reflecting on his move from Denver. "That is, with the exception of Frank McGuire and his wife, Pat. They were such outstanding people, I could hardly wait to come. When I did, Frank took such a personal interest. He spent days helping me find a house and was just so nice."

In many ways, Smith and McGuire were an odd couple, but

their efforts guided the Tar Heels to three of their best records. Only 27 years old when he accepted his new position, Smith's upbringing in the Phog Allen school made him concerned with every detail. With this background in strict, fundamental training, he was prepared to see that the Tar Heels' practice sessions followed a similar direction. But McGuire, the cagey veteran, tried not to overpractice or tell his players too many things to do. Always cool and calm, he was a great believer in recruiting outstanding athletes, then allowing them to play their brand of basketball. He sought talent, and upon getting his share, he stressed a freelance offensive style. "We were very different," McGuire recollected, "but I ran the show. That's always the way it has been with me. I listened to my assistants, and I listened to Dean; but I called the shots. We had guys like York Larese and Doug Moe, guys who were street-smart from playing basketball on the New York playgrounds and who adjusted to whatever happened out there on the court. I let them play, and this was just not what Dean had been accustomed to at Kansas under Phog Allen."

Smith displayed his competitive fire to McGuire early in their relationship. "I will always remember our playing handball," McGuire said. "Dean had only played once before, and I beat him, but there he would be, scrambling around and diving all over the floor trying to win. He never thinks he is beaten and is the same way in golf. He'll hit a bad shot, then scramble back for par. He keeps trying, and that is important because that quality is reflected by his players. I love to see them. They are just like Dean was then, diving and never quitting."

Working with the Tar Heel defense was probably Smith's largest contribution under McGuire. "Dean's defense has always been a big thing," McGuire said. "He brought it with him from Kansas." Smith felt his defensive training was a key factor in getting the job at North Carolina. "The fact that our defenses had been so successful at Kansas might have been why I was hired at Carolina, because our '52 team did press St. John's [then coached by McGuire] in the finals." McGuire, while not implying that the defensive tradition at Kansas was the main reason for Smith's hiring, did agree that Smith's education in defense had been a good one. "They taught more defense out there in the Midwest than we did in the East in those days," McGuire said. "Dean knew all the stances and switches; he was really a solid defensive man."

So solid, in fact, that McGuire often wondered at his assistant's obsession with defense. It seemed Smith was setting up defenses in his sleep, even dreaming about defense. "There is this humorous story about Dean," McGuire said. "We were on the road once and were sharing a room. I was asleep, but kind of halfway woke up with a feeling that someone was standing over my bed. I turned over and was scared almost to death. There was Dean, hovering in his defensive stance. He has since broken the habit, but he did some sleepwalking back then. Anyway, he made a little move, then went back to bed—always thinking defense."

Smith seemed to be on the run constantly, trying to learn about basketball. He begged McGuire to let him do more. "I was going to let the young man take his time and get adjusted," McGuire said, "and here he was, wanting desperately to work."

It was not long before Smith had more responsibility than he bargained for. After only three years as McGuire's assistant and five full seasons as an aide on the college level, Smith was suddenly thrust into the position of heading one of the nation's top programs. Following a 19–4 season, McGuire decided in August 1961 to move to a head-coaching post with a professional team, the Philadelphia Warriors of the National Basketball Association. "There was no more challenge for me in college basketball," McGuire said in explaining his decision, "and I wanted the chance to coach Wilt." Wilt "the Stilt" Chamberlain was the fantastic seven-foot-one all-NBA performer who had played on the strong Kansas team nipped by McGuire's Tar Heels in three overtimes for the 1957 NCAA championship.

McGuire's choice for his successor was clear-cut. His opin-

Smith and former UNC Chancellor William Aycock
outside the Smith Center

Photo by Hugh Morton

ion was well respected, but even so, UNC Chancellor William Aycock asked the departing coach if he did not want to think about his recommendation for a week or so. "I said no," McGuire remembered, "and I convinced Chancellor Aycock that Dean could do the job. [Aycock had come to know Smith well during the NCAA hearings that resulted in probation for the North Carolina program. And he actually wanted Smith hired.] But I had to convince Dean, too. He really didn't want the job."

While serving his apprenticeship under McGuire, Smith had been getting offers to be head coach at other schools. Following his first year at North Carolina, he had been asked by Coach Hoyt Brawner to visit the University of Denver. "I got as far as Raleigh-Durham Airport," Smith recalled, "but called Hoyt from the airport and said I had changed my mind at that time. After my second year at Chapel Hill, Dick Harp called and said, 'Come to Kansas as my assistant. After four to seven years, I'll be retiring, and the head-coaching job will be yours.' I didn't think I could assist Dick because I couldn't disagree with him. I still looked on him as my coach. Also, Coach McGuire took me on a recruiting trip, got me up to New York, and in that charming way of his said, 'You don't want to go to Kansas, do you?' I said no. And then Ben Carnevale was telling me I could have the Navy job." Smith didn't want any of those positions at that point in his career, and he did not yearn for the Tar Heel post either.

Smith was flattered at being handpicked by such a highly regarded basketball man as McGuire, but he sincerely hoped his boss would remain as head basketball coach at North Carolina. Also, Hoyt Brawner had by then revealed to Smith that he planned to retire after another year as coach at the University of Denver to become that school's athletic director, and he encouraged Dean to feel that the coaching position would be his. Smith planned to accept and move back to a familiar area closer to his home state.

"No, Dean didn't want the job at all," McGuire remembered. "But I told Chancellor Aycock and I told Dean, too, that he could handle it. He was the man for the position, and I knew what he could do. I saw a great career ahead for him. Sure, he was young, but I had no doubts about his ability."

Smith tried to persuade McGuire to remain with the Tar Heels. He once thought he and Pat McGuire had succeeded, but McGuire changed his mind again and accepted the Philadelphia offer.

Smith well remembers his naive beginnings in his new post. "I didn't even know what recruiting was, and I didn't think I was ready," he said. "But I can still see Frank driving me over to Chancellor Aycock's. Frank went in for a while, and when he came out, he said, 'Congratulations, Dean, you're the new basketball coach.' Just like that."

Smith, UNC Athletic Director Chuck Erickson,
and Frank McGuire

The fact that McGuire went to the chancellor to recommend
Smith caused an awkward situation. "Chuck Erickson was the
athletic director," Smith said, "and there was talk he wanted a
former Carolina player, Dan Nyimicz, to get the coaching job.
I'm not really sure about that, but I don't think Chuck was
happy about not being consulted or given a chance to help
pick the new coach. Frank, though, was showing his loyalty
to me and wanted to make sure I was named coach. Chancellor Aycock also wanted me to be the coach."

Smith was extremely young for a head coach of a big-time
college basketball team, especially in an era when experience
and age were considered vital factors. Though only 30, he was
far ahead of most coaches the same age. After all, he had been
hanging around basketball courts since he was old enough to

walk; he had heard his father discussing basketball's finer points as long as he could remember; and he had even done a bit of coaching while a player at Kansas University. He had only five years' formal experience in college basketball coaching, but Smith had been on the coaching scene most of his life.

Nevertheless, his task was not to be an easy one. Smith had the advantage of inheriting a winning program, but he was also inheriting a shadow—the rather imposing shadow of Frank McGuire. Popular, dashing, and brimming with charisma, McGuire was a difficult act to follow. The Tar Heels had not won fewer than 18 games in a season during Smith's three years on the staff, and McGuire's NCAA championship five years earlier had left UNC alumni with a sweet taste in their mouths, one difficult for a mere mortal like Smith to satisfy. Before he ever sat at his desk, Smith was being viewed with raised eyebrows; he had a great deal to live up to.

"Frank gave me some very good advice," Smith said, "advice I regret not having taken. He told me to do something different, to make a change of some kind. Change the uniforms or change the bench, just do something, something to let people know I was the coach, that Frank McGuire wasn't any longer; that was his idea. I didn't do it, but I should have."

If Smith didn't have enough of a load to shoulder, North Carolina had just been hit with NCAA probation. According to the NCAA enforcement office, UNC was guilty of "providing entertainment to prospects and parents of prospects and for excessive aid to student-athletes." The school was penalized by being prohibited from participating in the NCAA Tournament for one year. In addition, the University of North Carolina limited the Tar Heels to 14 conference games and two nonleague games and to two basketball scholarships outside the geographical area of the ACC for the 1961–62 season. "The recruiting limitations would have the biggest impact," Smith said. "I remember [North Carolina State Coach] Everett Case telling me that the real problem would be three years later."

Dean Smith was a man on the spot. After the graduation of all-Americans Doug Moe and York Larese, there were only four players coming back from the 19–4 team of the year before, among them guards Larry Brown and Donnie Walsh and forward Jim Hudock. Not a single player on the 14-man Tar Heel squad was taller than six-foot-seven, and only one could dunk the ball. Needless to say, there was a shortage of rebounding strength. After finishing at .500 for the regular season, North Carolina was eliminated in the first round of the ACC Tournament, giving Smith an 8–9 record in his initial test as a head coach. The high point of the season was a sound whipping of Notre Dame, 99–80; but after being accustomed to nearly 20 wins a season, some North Carolina fans were disappointed at failing to reach double figures in the victory column. Many, though, were tickled with the team's wins over Notre Dame and North Carolina State. Smith was pleased. "Considering everything, I thought we had a pretty good year," he said. "We did a good job with the people we had. Of course, it would have been fun to win more, but we played some tough teams. The ACC schedule is always rugged, and outside opponents were Indiana and Notre Dame, both of them strong."

Smith remembers being so nervous during his first game as head coach "that I forgot my own tired signal. I had told the players to raise their fists when tired, and I would get a substitute in for them. Well, Larry Brown and Donnie Walsh both raised their fists, and I just yelled out at them, 'Go get 'em, boys.'"

History was made as Smith suffered the only losing season of his career, yet North Carolina fans were generally understanding of the circumstances under which their new coach was working. "At the time, I didn't think of things as being so difficult," Smith said. "People were nice to me, especially the people who mattered. Their kindness made things much easier. Chancellor Aycock said to me, 'Get the best young men you can,' and basically told me I had my job as long as there were no NCAA probations, no gambling, and no fights."

Smith was also treated quite kindly by North Carolina State Coach Everett Case, known as "the Silver Fox." "Everett was so nice to me," Smith said. "I'd go over to his house, and we'd sometimes stay up until two in the morning talking basketball. He'd tell me stories, and I was a very interested listener. Those are fond memories. The first time we played him after I became head coach, Carolina won, and Everett was as gracious as he could be. The next time, State held the ball and beat us. After the game, Everett winked at me and said, 'The old Fox taught you a lesson.' I asked what he meant, and he said, 'You can hold the basketball.' He was wonderful to me."

The world of head coaching was entirely different from what Smith had experienced as an assistant; but even though there was a period of adjustment, he never looked very far ahead and never set any timetables for getting his program in gear. "I don't think I even thought in those terms," he said. "I was 30 years old and anxious to teach, to get on the court, and to play games. I didn't really realize what it took to be a head coach."

When discussing his early shortcomings, Smith talks about the importance of recruiting. "The best example came during my first year," he said. "We could sign only two players from outside our area, and I thought we had better go for size because there weren't any big North Carolinians that year. So we recruited a lot of big guys; and one, Bob Bennett, who was six-foot-seven-and-a-half, wrote us in February and said he was interested in Carolina. We found out later that the time Bennett wrote us was the same time Duke had more or less said to him that Jack Marin, who was about the same size as Bennett, was going to Duke. Bob was still offered a scholarship at Duke, but Marin going there kind of made Bennett look elsewhere. But I was thrilled to sign someone his size and with his intellect and ability."

Since the New York connection had taken care of recruiting when McGuire was coaching the Tar Heels, Smith was not accustomed to going out in search of players. "I had no idea what recruiting was about when I was at [the] Air Force Academy," Smith said. "Bob Spear and I tried to cover the entire country just by writing letters; and once in a while, we'd get to meet an athlete face-to-face. But there were no campus visits in those days for the recruits. Then, coming to Chapel Hill, I didn't do any recruiting because Frank had his friend Harry Gotkin in New York. I'd go out and see a high school game locally now and then, but most of our players came from New York. I remember the first time Frank ever let me go to New York on a so-called recruiting trip. I arrived up there in April 1959. Harry met me at the airport and said, 'Let's go over here and see this team.' He said, 'We've got this player and this one,' and named off five players. The five were Art Heyman, Larry Brown, Dick Brennan, Kenny McIntyre, and Billy Galantai. Harry added, 'All five are set. They're going to Carolina.' I said, 'Great, Harry,' and that was the recruiting trip." UNC actually got only two of those players, Brown and Galantai, the latter after attending a Wilmington, North Carolina, prep school along with Brennan and McIntyre. Heyman wound up an all-American at Duke.

"A recruiting experience which was kind of a funny one involved a young man named Steve Vacendak. He had come down from Pennsylvania and visited us in the fall of his senior year of high school. So, naturally, I couldn't understand when spring came and Steve didn't pick Carolina; he chose Duke instead. Vic Bubas, the Duke coach, taught us all that you have to stay after these recruits by writing them all the time. The Duke staff was calling or visiting the Vacendak family all along. This just showed me that, gosh, you have to stay with this thing, this recruiting. I had even gone down to the Gator Bowl one year to watch our football team. I like football, but I wouldn't begin to do that now. One can't do that sort of thing in this job. Frank had people out working at getting players for him. I didn't."

Today, the North Carolina basketball office in the Smith Center includes separate offices for Smith and assistants Bill Guthridge, Phil Ford, Dave Hanners, and Randy Wiel. There are four full-time secretaries. The furnishings are comfortable. Smith's office walls are lined with photos of his former players. There are basketballs autographed by Carolina teams, and on a coffee table is an ashtray inscribed with the scores of games and the names of players from the UNC teams of 1966– 69. Smith hasn't used it since he stopped smoking.

His first office wasn't nearly as spacious or attractive. "I had talked Frank into enlarging it," Smith said, "so we had two offices then and even enough room for a secretary. Betsy Terrell was the secretary, and she ran the show while I was on the road. I was called in once by Chuck Erickson and our faculty chairman, Dr. E. M. Hedgpeth. They told me I spent too much on phone calls, even more than the chancellor. I said, 'I hope so; the chancellor isn't in the business of recruiting.'"

Smith's second season at North Carolina, 1962–63, was a fine one, led by a sophomore jumping jack nicknamed "the Kangaroo Kid." He was Billy Cunningham, destined to become a college all-American and an all-pro in both the National Basketball Association and the now-defunct American Basketball Association. Cunningham averaged 22.7 points and 16.1 rebounds per game that year, the latter figure belying his height of six-foot-four-and-a-half, quite short for his position as center. Cunningham received ample support from the backcourt of Larry Brown (a future Olympian and all-ABA performer and a coach on both the pro and college levels) and Yogi Poteet, both of whom averaged over 13 points.

The Tar Heels jumped to a quick start with wins in six of their first seven games, one of the triumphs coming over perennial power Kentucky at Lexington and another over Notre

Dame at South Bend. A one-point loss to Wake Forest in the ACC Tournament closed the door on a 15–6 season, one that would have had an excellent chance of producing 20 wins if North Carolina had played as many games as most other college teams. The Tar Heel team might have been exceptional had Cunningham gotten more help on the backboards. His front-court partners, both North Carolinians, were six-foot-four Ray Respess and six-foot-three Morehead Scholar Charlie Shaffer. The team's winning percentage of .714 was only a hint of what could be expected from Smith-coached teams in the future.

It was Smith's third year at the Carolina helm that he feels was his worst season as a coach. The Tar Heels ended at 12–12 and were inconsistent. Inconsistency, Smith believes, was also his main problem as a coach that season. "The first two years, everything was fine," he said, "but that third year . . . well, that was the only time I thought we were back to relying on hope. I couldn't make up my mind which guys to play. Here we had Cunningham and a group of other fine players who were all about equal in ability. I kept shuffling players and changing my lineup. I'd say it was the worst coaching job of my career. We had a slump in February, losing six of our last seven games of the regular season. I tried everything, but I shouldn't have."

Typical of Smith, though, was the fact that he built on a negative experience. "It helped me say to myself, 'Okay, I'm not going to change the lineup much.' Athletes are secure when they are playing regularly. But anytime you have a guy looking over his shoulder, saying, 'Hey, if I make a mistake, somebody else is going to start the next game,' it does something to that player so that he just can't concentrate on his job. Now, our substitution system is based on security. Looking back, based on the people we had, we should have had 15 or 16 wins instead of 12." Despite the disappointments, there was again the shining performance of Cunningham, who

Billy Cunningham

averaged 26 points while soaring for 15.8 rebounds per contest, both ACC-leading averages.

Such glowing statistics made Cunningham an all-American choice as a junior and a preseason selection for numerous honors his senior season, 1964–65. Another promising Tar Heel was sophomore sensation Bob Lewis, who had wowed North Carolina fans with a 36.6 scoring average in freshman competition. (The NCAA did not allow first-year collegians to participate in varsity basketball or football until 1972.) With two exceptional athletes, Carolina fans predicted a bright season for their Tar Heels. Such great expectations proved to be a real problem.

"Looking at Cunningham and Lewis on the same team, everybody thought, 'Hey, we're back in business here at Carolina,'" Smith reflected. "It wasn't that easy. For one thing, there was too much buildup and too much pressure on Lewis. That's why I have the approach today of freshmen not talking to the press until after they have played a game for Carolina. Bobby had a great sophomore year [21 points per game], but people didn't think so because of his stats as a freshman, when he was a six-three center. But those stats came against teams not nearly as strong as Bobby would face on the varsity, so the figures were misleading. The competition had changed drastically. People tend to look too much at numbers and not enough at where those numbers come from. I was as guilty as anyone of building up Bobby; I overdid it. But from that point on, I haven't built up first-year players."

The opening 12 games of the 1964–65 season saw North Carolina with six wins and six losses. It was during the worst period of this up-and-down start that Smith was shown a bizarre act of nonsupport by a group of students. On a cold January night, the Tar Heels were returning to Chapel Hill from Winston-Salem, where they had been soundly defeated 107–85 by ACC opponent Wake Forest, marking their fourth straight loss. To demonstrate their dissatisfaction, several students gathered in front of old Woollen Gym, then in its final year as UNC's home court. As the bus carrying the Tar Heels slowed to a stop on South Road, the players and coaches could hardly believe their eyes. There, on an old oak tree just to the right of the gym, a lynching was taking place, as the students were hanging Dean Smith in effigy. Shock was quickly displaced by anger among the players, but Smith remained characteristically unnerved.

Jimmy Smithwick, a junior on the squad, recalled the incident this way: "A lot of the guys were seething, but Coach Smith was calm and walked up to the front of the bus. He said, 'Fellas, you don't have anything to be ashamed of. Don't worry about this kind of thing. Just hold your heads up and walk out of this bus like gentlemen. I don't expect one word out of any of you.'"

Ignoring the scene was not quite so easy for Billy Cunningham, however. The Tar Heel star charged into the crowd of students and tore down the dummy of Smith. Several teammates followed in support. "It's tough to ignore someone being hung in effigy," Cunningham said. "It was just so unfair because Coach Smith had done everything he possibly could do as a coach. We just didn't have the personnel to be a real good basketball team. Under the circumstances, he did a fine job. We were just a so-so team, and at that time Coach Smith was coming under a lot of heat and pressure from the alumni. Everyone was expecting Carolina basketball to be what it had been earlier, without the talent and without being able to recruit. It was almost an impossible situation."

Today, Smith can find a silver lining in the episode. "When Cunningham ripped down the dummy," he said, "I acted as if I didn't see it. . . . Anyway, two days later, we went over to Durham for our next game and upset Duke, which was going great in its heyday and ended the season ranked in the top 10 in both major polls. So I'm glad those students did what they did because what happened certainly gave us an emotional edge for the Duke game."

After splitting their next four games, the Tar Heels won

seven in a row to enter the ACC Tournament with high hopes. Those hopes were shattered quickly, however, a 16-point shellacking at the hands of Wake Forest putting the lid on a 15–9 season.

Smith suffered additional frustrations during the 1964–65 season. "There were the expectations of the fans, the bad start, and then the winning streak, which had everyone thinking we were going to win the tournament," he recalled. "We lost in the first round, ending the year poorly. There was some pressure; but by then, I was dealing with it. I'd say that season was the toughest for me. I think I was worrying too much during it.

"I was beginning to do a lot of free reading late at night, and around January of that season, I was reading Catherine Marshall's book *Beyond Our Selves*. There was this one chapter in the book about the power of helplessness which was really meaningful for me at that point in my life. As I read the book, I said to myself that maybe I shouldn't be coaching. And to myself, or in prayer, I said, 'I'm healthy; I could do a lot of things. So, why worry?' I think I was more relaxed all of a sudden and had more peace of mind. Even though we started winning, I certainly don't believe in prayer having anything to do with winning or losing. However, as a result of reading that book and [as a result of] that prayer, I was able to put things into perspective. That has always meant a lot to me. I'm not going to get uptight about one game anymore."

Cunningham graduated, having repeated as an all-American and having led the ACC with averages of 25.4 points and 14.3 rebounds his senior year. No one player could replace a talent like the Kangaroo Kid, but a six-foot-three sophomore named Larry Miller arrived to partially fill the void. Miller scored 20.9 points a game and Bob Lewis added 27.4 to lead North Carolina to a 16–11 record in 1965–66.

One of the highlights of that season would not be realized for its true impact until years later—North Carolina's adoption of the four-corners offense as a delay game. It was used

Larry Brown with members of the 1965–66 Tar Heel
freshman team. Kneeling are Gerald Tuttle and
Dick Grubar. Standing are Jim Bostick, Bill Bunting,
Rusty Clark, and Joe Brown.

very effectively in an 82–72 triumph at Ohio State, but more extensively in a 21–20 loss to Duke in the ACC Tournament semifinals. Smith had his Tar Heels in the four corners from the outset and almost managed an upset of a much stronger Blue Devil team. Greatly outmanned, the Tar Heels simply dared Duke to chase them, with walk-on Johnny Yokley the key ball handler. That game was the first time basketball fans took notice of the unusual delay offense, but it would not be the last.

Meanwhile, the Tar Heel freshman team was winning 15 of 16 games under Smith's protégé, Larry Brown. Leading that team was the first legitimate big man Smith would coach, six-ten-and-a-half Rusty Clark from Fayetteville, North Carolina. There were also six-foot-eight Bill Bunting, slick playmaker Dick Grubar, and solid, if not spectacular, Joe Brown and Gerald Tuttle. That quintet would become an integral part of the North Carolina varsity as sophomores and would form the nucleus of a team that would accomplish much its next three years.

Dean Smith had compiled a 66–47 record during his first five years at Chapel Hill. He had his feet firmly on the ground now, and the glory years were on the horizon.

TWENTY-FOUR-CARAT GOLD

Chapel Hill is a quaint little town nestled among the pines of North Carolina's prominent Research Triangle area, with Durham only a three-point shot away and Raleigh within a full-court pass. Referred to by University of North Carolina graduates as "the southern part of heaven," it is a typical college town. The UNC campus is a pleasant mix of rich tradition and natural beauty. The older buildings are covered with blankets of ivy, and when the canopy of dogwood trees blossoms each spring, the picture painted is a masterpiece.

The University of North Carolina has an enrollment of nearly 23,000 students. Its business and journalism programs and its nursing school are renowned, and its law and medical schools are considered among the best in the nation. On the main campus is an age-old central meeting place called the Old Well, the university's trademark. Old buildings are interlaced with modern structures, creating a checkerboard blend.

Among other luminaries, Carolina has produced author

Thomas Wolfe and well-known television commentator Charles Kuralt. While maintaining a solid academic reputation, the university has more than held its own in athletics. Several sports have had their moments in the sun, but basketball is the favorite game in town. It is as much a part of Chapel Hill tradition as ivy and the Old Well. In fact, folks from the immediate area, as well as alumni and fans of the school, practically live for the roundball season to roll in. Tickets for Tar Heel home games are hot items, even with the seating capacity more than doubled since the Smith Center replaced Carmichael Auditorium.

The 1966–67 season marked the dawn of Dean Smith's glory years at North Carolina. The stage had been set almost two years earlier, when the Tar Heel coach enjoyed a bonanza recruiting haul. Smith had already proven he could successfully court high school stars when he signed Bob Lewis and Larry Miller, but he had not brought in a number of quality players in one recruiting crop. The group of athletes in the 1965–66 freshman basketball class, however, furnished Smith with several ingredients that had been missing in his five years at the UNC helm.

First and foremost was height, an absolute must for grabbing missed shots off the backboards and triggering fast breaks. Smith's initial big man with talent came in a six-ten-and-a-half package with a shock of red hair.

He was Franklin Clark, better known as Rusty. As a senior, Rusty Clark had led Fayetteville Senior High School to the North Carolina state championship. And he carried academic credentials impressive enough to earn him the Morehead Scholarship, a prestigious grant awarded by the university. During his career as a Tar Heel, Clark would always be underrated. He would also be at his most productive in the most crucial games. Of Clark, Smith would later say, "When I got Rusty, people started saying, 'Hey, that Smith can really coach.' I will always have him to thank for so much."

Another essential ingredient was chemistry, a unique blend

Rusty Clark

Smith with Larry Miller, Bill Bunting,
Rusty Clark, and Dick Grubar

of personnel that included the qualities of leadership, un-selfishness, and a willingness to pay the price necessary to attain lofty heights.

The remainder of that Tar Heel freshman cast meshed well with Clark. There was Dick Grubar, who had been a six-foot-four center at his high school in Schenectady, New York. Duke Assistant Coach Chuck Daly, now of the Detroit Pistons, had called Grubar too slow, but Grubar proved quick enough to become Carolina's point guard. He offered leader-ship and tough defense; and while he did not score often, he seemed to have a knack for coming up with clutch points. His greatest assets were his abilities to fill the floor general's role and to hit open teammates with crisp passes. Bill Bunting was a six-foot-eight, pencil-thin quiet man from New Bern, North Carolina. His father had attended Duke, located in Durham, only eight miles from Chapel Hill. Bunting combined excep-tional quickness and a fine shooting touch. Helping supply depth were Joe Brown and Gerald Tuttle. The six-foot-five Brown, from Valdese, North Carolina, had been sought by many schools. He soon became the Tar Heels' valuable sixth man thanks to his aggressive performances off the bench. Tuttle, a five-foot-eleven guard from London, Kentucky, was easily signed. He was able to enter a game in the toughest of situations and take charge of the offense while strengthening the defense. As Smith said, "We couldn't have asked for a better situation, a better chemistry, but that's luck. It just worked out that way."

Clark, Grubar, Bunting, Brown, and Tuttle had proven a brilliant team as freshmen, but they faced the gargantuan challenge of the ACC wars as varsity rookies. Solidifying the group were Larry Miller and Bob Lewis, the latter an all-American selection. Both could score points in bunches, and they owned valuable experience. Most importantly, they fused well with the newcomers.

Smith was optimistic at the start of the 1966–67 season. Beginning his sixth year as UNC head coach, he said, "This is the first time since I've been here that we have had enough depth that all positions are up for grabs."

That optimism was rewarded with immediate results, as the Tar Heels won their first nine games and 16 of the first 17. Of particular significance was a road victory over Kentucky, a national power under the fabled Adolph Rupp and a team that had finished as national runner-up the previous season. Carolina demonstrated that it could win close, hard-fought struggles, and it also displayed the capacity for delivering the knockout punch, blowing away a number of foes on the way to the ACC regular-season championship.

In those days, conferences were allowed to send only one team into the NCAA playoffs. In the ACC, the conference tournament winner was declared the champion and awarded a trip to the NCAA tourney. The ACC Tournament was therefore packed with pressure. It remains filled with excitement because of the rivalries within the league, but the precious playoff berth that hinged on the tourney's outcome added more electricity in days gone by.

By tournament time in 1967, Carolina's rookies were veterans with 25 games under their belts. They responded well behind the play of Miller, who was voted the ACC Tournament's most valuable player. Miller was unstoppable in the title game win over Duke. The junior with a guard's size and a forward's strength hit 13 of 14 floor shots en route to 32 points. His coach recalled something that might have inspired Miller: "The Greensboro papers helped us a little. Even though we had beaten Duke twice during the season, there were stories saying Duke was still favored in the tournament. Larry took it personally, had a great tournament, then presented the clippings to the writers." Bob Lewis added 26 points in the championship game.

The Tar Heels then avenged an early-season loss to Princeton by defeating the Tigers in the East Regional semifinals. They won the championship by easily toppling Boston College. Carolina thus found itself among the final four teams

Larry Miller drives to the basket against Virginia Tech

vying for the national title, but lopsided losses to Dayton in the NCAA semifinals and Houston in the consolation game pulled the plug on an otherwise bright season. Nonetheless, the Tar Heels were back in the collegiate basketball spotlight.

Smith was recognized for a 26–6 season by being named ACC coach of the year, while placing third in the balloting for national coach of the year. The 36-year-old coach from Kansas was beginning to be noticed, and his North Carolina basketball team was just starting to make heads turn. The Tar Heels finished third and fourth, respectively, in the Associated Press and United Press International national rankings. It was the first of a long string of outstanding seasons. Smith was rekindling a rich basketball tradition and ushering in the most prosperous era in the school's roundball history.

The 1967–68 season brought sophomore Charlie Scott, a New York City native who arrived in Chapel Hill by way of Laurinburg Institute, a predominantly black prep school in eastern North Carolina. A six-foot-five, silk-smooth operator with a fluid jump shot and amazing all-around ability, Scott was a gem. He became the first black scholarship athlete at the University of North Carolina, putting him in the proverbial fishbowl. He joined Vanderbilt's Perry Wallace as the first black Division I athletes on scholarship in the South. They entered college the same year, and everyone was watching.

The Great Scott, as he came to be called in the ACC, or Charles, as Smith referred to him, did not disappoint anyone. Scott faced some verbal abuse during road games, as expected, but he patiently weathered the storm. Meanwhile, he performed sensationally after adjusting to the rigors of being a rookie in the major-college basketball arena and learning to fit his phenomenal talents into Smith's team-play style, which has never been altered for even the most gifted athletes. With all-American Miller, Clark, Grubar, and company still around, the pressure on Scott to produce was minimal.

Although his team was blessed with considerable talent, Smith was concerned entering the 1967–68 campaign. "This

Larry Brown with Charlie Scott and Eddie Fogler

was the first time everyone was really shooting at us," he said, "and I was worried some about our players getting cocky." The Tar Heels won twice, then lost at Vanderbilt, which was in the top 10 at the time. "I remember I had a locker-room meeting with the team after the Vandy game," Smith said. "That, by the way, was the last one of those meetings I've had, because it's easy to become too emotional after a game; and one may not be so rational. Anyway, I wasn't really angry, but we talked about the way we were playing, which wasn't too good. I boarded a single-engine plane with our broadcasting crew, and we headed over the mountains of Tennessee in a hailstorm. It was rough, and Richard Raley, the engineer for the broadcasters, said, 'Let's just get out of this.' All of a sudden, that's what I was thinking about, too, and other things didn't matter so much."

Carolina bounced back with wins over Kentucky and Princeton, both top-10 teams. Those triumphs started a winning streak that stretched to 20 games, including the championship of the Far West Classic and victories in 12 successive ACC contests. With a second straight regular-season title tucked away, the Tar Heels also made it two ACC Tournaments in a row by blitzing rival North Carolina State in the most one-sided title game in tourney history, 87–50. Miller was again the tournament MVP, scoring 31, 24, and 31 points in the three games.

In the opening game of the East Regional, the Tar Heels faced an undefeated St. Bonaventure outfit led by Bob Lanier, a six-eleven physical specimen who was much bigger and stronger than his Tar Heel counterpart, Rusty Clark. A prolific scorer, Lanier was considered to be more than the UNC junior redhead could handle. Clark proceeded to surprise everyone except Smith, who had been praising his pivotman's efforts for two years. Clark outplayed Lanier decisively in the game's early stages, allowing the Tar Heels to pull away to an insurmountable lead. Clark finished with 18 points and 10 rebounds, with Lanier getting 23 points and nine boards. But

Smith and the Tar Heels celebrate
winning the 1968 East Regional

the Bonnie star picked up most of his statistics after the contest had already been decided. Miller scored 27 points and Scott added 21, but Clark was the hero. North Carolina notched its second straight trip to the Final Four by defeating Davidson, with Clark earning the East Regional MVP award after scoring 22 points and grabbing 17 rebounds.

Bill Bunting, a steady player normally overlooked by the press and the fans, but not by his teammates and the coaching staff, sparked Carolina to a quick start over Ohio State in the national semifinals. The thin man was a demon on the boards, snatching 12 rebounds, while Clark pulled down 11. All five Tar Heel starters scored in double figures, Miller and Bunting leading the way with 20 and 17. An 80–66 victory sent UNC into the championship game.

Lurking was the most powerful college basketball machine

of all time, the UCLA Bruins. UCLA was in the midst of a dynastic era that would produce 10 national titles in a span of 12 years, seven in succession. The Bruins had everything. They were coached by "the Wizard of Westwood," John Wooden. Making them practically unbeatable was the incomparable Lew Alcindor, the seven-one center who was so agile, so intimidating, and so talented; known today as Kareem Abdul-Jabbar, he recently retired as the NBA's all-time leading scorer. The guards were twin lightning bolts Mike Warren and Lucius Allen. North Carolina was not favored to win, and it did not.

Smith's ploy was to shrink the game by taking 30 seconds or so off the clock on each possession. Carolina stayed close, trailing by only six points with 17 minutes left, before UCLA blew the game open and won 78–55. Alcindor finished with 34 points and 16 rebounds. "In my opinion, that was the best college team of all time," the UNC coach said.

North Carolina's 28–4 record earned Smith a second straight ACC coach-of-the-year honor. As a token of their appreciation, Tar Heel fans presented him with a Carolina-blue Cadillac. Reluctantly, yet graciously, he said, "I'm simply not the Cadillac type. I will accept the gift, though, because I think it is a symbol of the admiration for our players and assistant coaches and all they have accomplished. In that spirit, I will be very proud to drive it."

Gone for the 1968–69 season was Miller, who had certainly lived up to the lofty expectations accompanying his arrival at UNC. Still, folks had come to expect big things from Smith and his Tar Heels, and the loss of a superstar didn't change that.

Carolina did not disappoint its fans. The club had experience in facing a demanding schedule and postseason pressure, so there was savvy to go along with the talent. The seniors on the squad contributed the kind of leadership Smith had come to expect of his final-year players.

Another fast start included a third win in as many years

Smith in his Carolina-blue Cadillac

over Kentucky, this one in Lexington—a feat few schools could boast at that time. The Tar Heels won 18 of their first 19 games and completed their regular season by losing to Duke, only their third setback against 22 wins. A few days later, Carolina and Duke were butting heads once more, this time for the ACC Tournament title and a trip to the NCAAs.

The Tar Heels had mashed Clemson in the tourney's opening round, then had come from behind to defeat Wake Forest in the semifinals. They trailed Duke by nine points at halftime of the finale, and with floor leader Grubar out with a knee injury, a third straight trip to the East Regional did not look promising. But Scott had saved some of the most dramatic heroics in the annals of the ACC Tournament for the second half. After scoring 23 points in the semis, Scott erupted in the championship game, sinking one long jump shot after another on the way to a 40-point show that included 17-of-23 accuracy from the floor. Riding the crest of Scott's torrid shooting, the Tar Heels beat the Blue Devils by 11.

Scott picked up in the East Regional where he had left off in the ACC Tournament, pouring in 22 points in Carolina's semifinal win over Duquesne. He then scored 32 in UNC's title-game win over Davidson, two of them on a late jumper that proved the game winner. Scott's heroics earned him MVP honors in his second straight tournament.

The Tar Heels were then bombed by Purdue in the NCAA semis and by Drake in the consolation game. UNC's final record was 27–5, and people in ACC country were starting to use the word *dynasty* when talking about North Carolina's basketball program. Clark, Bunting, Grubar, Tuttle, and Brown enjoyed the distinction of having played on three Atlantic Coast Conference and East Regional championship teams in as many years. In that period, the Tar Heels won 81 games, lost only 15, and were ranked no lower than fourth and as high as second in the nation.

Scott carried impressive credentials into 1969–70, his senior year, having averaged 22.3 points as a junior to earn numerous all-American honors. There wasn't much depth to the UNC team, but Smith had recruited another sound nucleus. The major figures were a pair of all-around forwards, six-foot-six Dennis Wuycik and six-foot-five Bill Chamberlain, along with hustling playmaker Steve Previs. The season produced 18 wins for the Tar Heels, a subpar total compared to the previous three years. Carolina lost its last three games, falling in the ACC Tournament's opening round to normally weak Virginia, then in the first round of the NIT. Scott averaged 27.1 points on the way to more all-American laurels.

With Scott gone, the Tar Heels were not predicted to do much in 1970–71. They were even picked to finish as low as seventh in the eight-team ACC. By the end of the season, however, Smith had more writers and fans singing his praises than ever before. The 1970–71 season was hailed as his best coaching job in 10 years at North Carolina. Counted out of the

Dennis Wuycik shoots against Clemson

ACC race before it even began, the Tar Heels charged to an 11–3 league record and another regular-season title. On the way, they won the hearts of fans with spirited efforts highlighted by totally unselfish teamwork, scrappiness, and all-out hustle. They narrowly missed the ACC Tournament championship, losing by a point to South Carolina on a bizarre, last-second jump ball that resulted in the deciding basket.

North Carolina accepted an invitation to the NIT. In the tournament opener, future pro superstar Julius "Dr. J" Erving of the University of Massachusetts was held in check by Dennis Wuycik's defense until the strong, consistent junior forward for the Tar Heels crumpled to the floor with a knee injury. UNC roared to a 41-point blitz of Massachusetts, then went on to win the NIT behind outstanding performances by Bill Chamberlain and Wuycik's replacement, Dave Chadwick, a soft-spoken minister's son. Chamberlain scored 24 points in the first-round win; Chadwick had 24 as the Tar Heels defeated Providence; and George Karl put in 21 to lead a semifinal victory over archrival Duke. Chamberlain then threw in 34 points and claimed tourney MVP honors as Carolina won the championship by easily racing past Georgia Tech.

Smith was voted ACC coach of the year for guiding the Tar Heels to a 26–6 season and the NIT title. There were those who felt he deserved even better than that. One of his admirers was Georgia Tech Coach Whack Hyder, who said, "I think Dean Smith was the best coach in America this year." The 1970–71 season was to have added significance as the years mounted. It stands as the first in a long string of seasons in which the Tar Heels have won at least 20 games.

Returning for the 1971–72 season was the core of the squad that had captured the NIT—Bill Chamberlain, George Karl, Steve Previs, Kim Huband, and Dennis Wuycik, his knee mended and sound again. Joining the team were Bobby Jones, a shy, six-foot-nine jumping jack, and six-foot-ten Bob McAdoo, a transfer from Vincennes Junior College. North

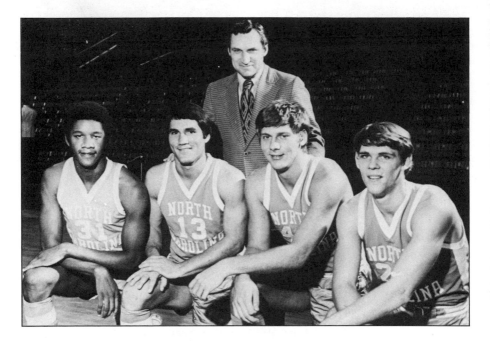

Smith with Bill Chamberlain, Steve Previs,
Dennis Wuycik, and George Karl

Carolina won five tournaments that season, plus the regular-season ACC championship. There was a 10-game winning streak along the way. UNC romped over Wake Forest and North Carolina State for the Big Four Tournament title, then captured the Sugar Bowl prize. Smith substituted freely, using 10 to 12 Tar Heels to keep fresh players on the court.

In the ACC Tournament, Smith's young men utilized quickness and defense to beat a tall, physical Maryland team for the title. Wuycik led the way with 24 points, and McAdoo was the tourney's MVP. North Carolina returned to the East Regional, cruising past South Carolina and Pennsylvania by a total of 37 points. Wuycik was named most valuable player. It was Smith's fourth East Regional championship in six years.

The Tar Heels next flew off to Los Angeles for the NCAA Final Four. With everyone looking for a Carolina-UCLA final,

Florida State proved a fly in the ointment. North Carolina fumbled and floundered early; meanwhile, the Seminoles were red-hot. UNC came alive in the second half, but Florida State had by then built a whopping lead, and they held on for a four-point upset win. The Tar Heels salvaged third place with a convincing victory over Louisville.

North Carolina finished 26–5, as Wuycik, who was selected an all-American, departed with fellow seniors Chamberlain, Previs, and Huband. The Tar Heels also suffered an unexpected loss, with McAdoo receiving an NBA offer he could not refuse. Smith did not try to persuade McAdoo to remain in Chapel Hill, but instead encouraged his all-American to negotiate the best contract he could with the Buffalo Braves. McAdoo had a chance to become an instant millionaire, and Smith emphasized that he would always advise his players to take advantage of such a rewarding opportunity. The UNC coach also saw to it that an incentive payment was written into the departing star's contract in the form of a bonus to be paid upon McAdoo's graduation from college.

For the next two years, North Carolina had to take a back seat to North Carolina State, the Wolfpack winning 57 of 58 games during that time. The Tar Heels were 25–8 in 1972–73, the season concluding with a victory in the NIT consolation contest.

The 1973–74 season was highlighted by what has come to be remembered as the most miraculous win in UNC basketball history. It took place during the last regular-season game. With a disappointed Carmichael Auditorium crowd beginning to pull on their jackets and coats to head for postgame dinners and parties, and with a regional television audience about to turn away from a game practically completed, Duke led Carolina 86–78. Only 17 seconds remained. Hardly anyone noticed when Bobby Jones made two free throws to reduce UNC's deficit to six. Walter Davis, a smooth, multitalented freshman, stole Duke's inbounds pass and fed John Kuester for a layup with 13 seconds on the clock, and the Blue

Walter Davis

Devil lead was four. The Tar Heels called a time-out, then continued to harass Duke with their pressing defense. The Devils mishandled the inbounds pass and lost it out of bounds. Davis missed a jumper, but Jones soared for the rebound and converted a layup with seven seconds left, slicing Duke's lead to 86–84. The Blue Devils finally got the ball inbounds, and Pete Kramer was fouled by Kuester. Kramer missed his free throw, and Ed Stahl rebounded for Carolina. Time-out was called with three seconds on the clock. The inbounds pass went to Davis, who looked for Jones. The Duke defense surrounded the Tar Heel leaper, so Davis dribbled past midcourt and let fly with a one-hander, the clock showing one second. The ball bounced off the glass and into the basket as the buzzer sounded. In overtime, Duke built a three-point lead before the Tar Heels rallied once more, finally winning 96–92 in one of the all-time exciting finishes in the ACC.

Carolina easily defeated Wake Forest in the opener of the conference tournament, then lost to a strong Maryland outfit in the semifinals. Another NIT trip was shortened as Purdue eliminated UNC in the opening round, putting the lid on a 22–6 season.

The 1974–75 Tar Heel team was a young one that raised many questions in preseason. How good would the rebounding be? Would the lack of experience hurt? Would there be any leadership in the backcourt? Was there enough outside shooting?

The last two questions were answered almost immediately by Phil Ford, a freshman whirling dervish from Rocky Mount, North Carolina. Ford had been a prolific scorer in high school, but few knew just how many other things he could do when turned loose in a basketball game. Before he was finished, this human dynamo would become the all-time leading scorer at UNC, as well as the school's top assist man.

The Tar Heels improved as the season wore on, much of the gradual progress in direct proportion to Ford's growing maturity as a floor leader. Carolina did not win more than four straight games until the very end of the season, but that was certainly the time to put together a winning streak. Included in UNC's seven regular-season losses were two defeats at the hands of North Carolina State, making eight successive times the Tar Heels had fallen to the Wolfpack after winning 11 in a row. Smith and his team finally applied the brakes to that skid, the victory igniting a spark that brought Carolina some surprising success.

In its final home game of the season, Carolina hosted David Thompson, Monte Towe, Tim Stoddard, and the rest of the team that had dominated the entire ACC for almost three years. Smith had seen his club come close to defeating the Wolfpack on several occasions, but the outcome continued to be the same. This time, the game was again close, but UNC was the victor by two points. Three days later, the Tar Heels accomplished another difficult task by downing Duke in the Blue Devils' Cameron Indoor Stadium in the traditional Duke-Carolina season-ender.

North Carolina entered the ACC Tournament with momentum, having knocked off its two biggest rivals the past week. Waiting for the Tar Heels in the opening round was their other Big Four foe, Wake Forest.

That game was to provide another miraculous finish, as the Demon Deacons led most of the contest and had an eight-point margin with 54 seconds remaining. Sparked by Dave Hanners's key steal, a pair of clutch jumpers by Brad Hoffman, and some sticky pressure defense, the Tar Heels stormed back to tie the score at the end of regulation time. A balanced offensive attack plus outstanding team defense in the game's crucial dying moments gave Carolina a 101–100 overtime win in one of the ACC Tournament's all-time thrillers. Walter Davis poured in 31 points and grabbed 12 rebounds; Ford added 25 points; Mitch Kupchak scored 16 and had 14 boards; and Hoffman contributed 15 points.

The semifinals saw North Carolina State edge Maryland,

while the Tar Heels again won in overtime, 76–71 over Clemson. Ford sank 15 of 18 free throws for 29 points, and Kupchak continued his strong board work with 15 rebounds.

In the championship clash, UNC built a six-point halftime lead and held on to win 70–66. Davis shadowed Thompson, his defense bothering the national player of the year to the extent that Thompson made only seven of 21 floor shots. Davis scored 14 points himself, Kupchak took down 12 rebounds, and Ford pumped in a game-high 24 points. More importantly, Ford ran the four corners to perfection, belying his freshman status by remaining unruffled in the contest's nerve-racking closing moments. As a reward, he was voted the tourney's most valuable player, a first for a freshman.

Syracuse ambushed the Tar Heels in the East Regional, staving off a patented Carolina finishing burst to win by two points. North Carolina then trounced Boston College in the consolation game to finish at 23–8, a fine accomplishment for a young team.

"It was a lot of fun," Smith said in reflecting on the season. "We won the tournament, and it had been awhile since we had done that. That year started all the four-corners business; but with Phil Ford in the middle, it really wasn't fair when we had the ball. He was that good."

Smith had used the four corners more than ever before during the 1974–75 season. The strategy was reliable, as Carolina hardly ever relinquished a lead. In fact, leads were often expanded. One reason was Ford and his amazing ability to penetrate opposing defenses. As the middle man in the spread offense, which came to be nicknamed the "Ford corners," he handled the ball most of the time and was fouled frequently. He seldom faltered at the free-throw line in crucial situations. The respect Ford commanded from North Carolina's opponents was itself a factor in the success of the four corners. When the defense overplayed Ford or his two teammates stationed in the corners near midcourt, the other two Tar Heels standing at the baseline had the opportunity to

Phil Ford

sneak behind the impatient defense. A crisp pass from Ford or one of the other ball handlers resulted in an easy layup. The four corners was an overwhelming success and caused much controversy. Disgruntled coaches complained that shooting clocks should be installed in college basketball, as they had been in the pros. No one could figure out how to stop the four corners, especially with a bolt of lightning like Ford in control.

Returning for the 1975–76 North Carolina season were almost all of the players responsible for the previous year's success. That and the fact that the Tar Heels had won the ACC title the year before led them to be picked to win the regular-season championship. They did just that, losing only once in 12 league games. They also went on a 13-game winning tear. There were two overtime victories over conference foes and six straight road triumphs, one of them a classic against Tulane in New Orleans, as the Tar Heels prevailed in four overtimes by a score of 113–106. Carolina received a bye in the opening round of the ACC Tournament. (The bye came about thanks to South Carolina's withdrawal from the Atlantic Coast Conference in 1971, which had left seven teams in the league. The addition of Georgia Tech brought ACC membership back to eight for the 1980 tourney.) The Tar Heels defeated Clemson in the semis, then were beaten by Virginia.

Still, North Carolina went to the NCAAs. The year before, the tournament field had been expanded by allowing some conferences to send more than one representative. Carolina was the ACC's at-large team in 1976, but Smith's club didn't last long. After playing so brilliantly during the regular season, the Tar Heels were mere ghosts of themselves against Alabama in the opening round. Ford had twisted his knee while playing in a pickup game in his hometown of Rocky Mount. He saw action against the Crimson Tide, but he hobbled noticeably and was ineffective. During the first half, John Kuester sustained what was later diagnosed as a broken foot. He continued to play, but he was slowed by the injury. The main factor, however, was Alabama center Leon Douglas,

Smith, John Thompson, Quinn
Buckner, and Mitch Kupchak during
the 1976 Olympics

Walter Davis in action with the
1976 Olympic team

who dominated the game in a 15-point Crimson Tide victory. The Tar Heels finished with a record of 25–4, good enough for the number-six spot in the final national rankings.

In terms of international recognition, Smith's greatest coaching accomplishment may have come when he directed the United States basketball team in the 1976 Olympics in Montreal. Considering the loss by the Americans in the 1972 Olympics in the game that has come to be known as "the Great Munich Court Robbery," the task was momentous. "This was the only time I ever felt my only job was to win," Smith said. "In fact, that's what I was told."

Smith had it difficult from the start. Criticism came as a result of player selections for the Olympic team, which included four Tar Heels and three other players from the Atlantic Coast Conference. Charges of partiality hounded Smith despite the fact that an Olympic selection committee, and not the head coach, was responsible for choosing the dozen athletes who would represent the United States. The Carolina players were Phil Ford, Mitch Kupchak, Walter Davis, and Tommy LaGarde, all of whom went on to play in the NBA. The other three ACC players were Maryland's Steve Sheppard, North Carolina State's Kenny Carr, and Duke's Tate Armstrong. Rounding out the American squad were Quinn Buckner and Scott May of Indiana, Tennessee's Ernie Grunfeld, Michigan's Phil Hubbard, and Notre Dame's Adrian Dantley.

Smith may not have chosen the team, but he did inform the selection committee as to what kind of players he wanted: quick athletes with defensive ability and plenty of desire. "I want guys who will hustle and play as a team," said Smith after the United States team had been named. "There isn't a man here who can't play offense, but that isn't what's going to win the gold medal for us."

In a very short time, Smith developed tremendous team proficiency among his Olympians, taking great individual talent and molding it into a squad as close-knit as a family.

Practice sessions were demanding, with the emphasis on defense and a running, aggressive offense. During exhibition games, Smith firmly reminded his players of the team concept whenever they drifted into playground basketball. The players took the cue and began believing. "Coach Smith is teaching us a lot real quickly," Adrian Dantley said. "If we play as a team, we'll win."

Dantley's assessment proved accurate. The Americans demonstrated complete unselfishness by the end of the practices, and unity overflowed onto the floor of the Montreal Forum. But it wasn't a cakewalk. "The only time I can remember feeling pressure before a game was before we played the Canadian team," Smith remembered. "There isn't supposed to be a home-court edge in the Olympics, and no team is supposed to have any more of a cheering section for a particular game than another; but Canada definitely had an advantage playing there in Montreal. I can't think of any game I've ever been more worried about." Six straight United States victories, among them a 95–77 triumph over Canada in the semifinals and a 95–74 triumph over Yugoslavia in the gold-medal game, silenced the critics—reporters, coaches whose players had been overlooked for the Olympic team, and second-guessers in general. Those who had followed Smith's success story at North Carolina were not surprised at his accomplishment.

The long weeks of hard work culminated when the medals were presented to the American players, as the entire team lined up for the ceremony and the national anthem. The coaches did not receive medals, but they enjoyed the same deep gratification as their players. "I never thought of myself as being terribly patriotic," Smith said, "but when I saw those guys getting their gold medals and when we all clutched each other—the other coaches, John Thompson and Bill Guthridge and I—well, it was one of those moments most people don't have. There were some tears and some very proud feelings." Smith said he received more satisfaction from seeing his team redeem itself in the face of widespread criticism than from the vindication of the traumatic 1972 loss.

Smith had done a magnificent job of coaching the Olympic team, but he made it clear that he did not want to return in the same capacity in 1980. "No, once is enough," he said. "Coaching our Olympic team was a great experience, but one others should have the opportunity to enjoy. We have many outstanding coaches in the United States, and others should have the chance."

The Olympic assignment made Smith's year a long one. His Carolina basketball season had begun back in October 1975 and ended in March. Then came the Olympic trials, practices, exhibition games, and finally the Olympics themselves. By the time the closing ceremonies rolled around, it was time to start planning for the 1976–77 Tar Heel season.

That season again saw the team fielding a predominantly veteran lineup, including the nucleus of Davis, LaGarde, Kuester, and Ford. Gone was all-American Mitch Kupchak, but helping to compensate for his loss were a half-dozen freshmen. Heading the group was Mike O'Koren, a six-foot-seven prep sensation from New Jersey. The season would be special in many ways. Carolina would go on to finish runner-up to national champion Marquette, but more remarkable was the manner in which that was accomplished. Despite being strapped by injuries to starters, UNC won big games down the stretch, with unsung heroes popping up everywhere.

After opening the season with a win over North Carolina State in the Big Four Tournament, the Tar Heels dropped a thriller to Wake Forest in the championship game. North Carolina went on to win 11 straight, three of those triumphs earning them the Far West Classic title. Carolina then lost three of its next four games, leaving its record at 13–4. With skeptics saying the bubble was bursting, UNC took off again. The Tar Heels built a 15-game winning streak, not losing another contest until the national championship game.

It wasn't easy, though. Tom LaGarde injured a knee during

practice early in the season and did not return. His backup, Jeff Wolf, underwent an appendectomy and was not at full strength for several weeks. Steve Krafcisin, like Wolf a freshman, was the next big man in line, and he injured a hip. The center's job then fell onto the shoulders of still another frosh, Rich Yonakor, a hustler who was more a forward than a pivotman.

In the ACC Tournament, Walter Davis broke the index finger on his shooting hand in a semifinal win over North Carolina State. John Kuester filled in for Ford, who fouled out in that victory. He ran the four corners extremely well and sank five crucial free throws in the closing minutes. Meeting Virginia in the finals for the second year in a row, the Tar Heels were hurting. Davis had fluid drained from his badly swollen finger before the game, and he saw only a few minutes of action. The Cavaliers were ahead by seven points with less than eight minutes remaining and were up by three when Ford fouled out with six minutes left. O'Koren later departed on fouls, leaving Kuester as the lone UNC regular on the court. He became the man of the hour and the tournament, directing the four corners and again hitting clutch foul shots as Carolina rallied for the championship. Scarcely noticed all season, Kuester was voted the tournament's most valuable player.

Smith paid tribute to his reserves' performance, saying, "I looked at our bench near the end [of the Virginia game] and saw all those starters. I couldn't help remembering all the talk about how weak our bench was. Well, that bench has been playing pretty well since the beginning of February."

The East Regional saw the Tar Heels continuing their battle against adversity. They came from behind in the second half to beat Notre Dame on St. Patrick's Day. Ford scored 29 points as UNC erased a 14-point deficit, but the junior guard hyperextended his right elbow in the game. Carolina then won the regional title by soundly whipping a bigger Kentucky outfit, countering the more physical Wildcats with quickness and

Walter Davis ices his broken finger, 1977 postseason

John Kuester celebrates his MPV award
after the 1977 ACC Tournament

defense, even though Ford played only 15 minutes and scored just two points. Kuester picked up the slack, dropping in 13 of 14 free throws to earn the regional's MVP award.

Looking very much like a team of destiny, North Carolina headed for Atlanta and the Final Four. Waiting in the NCAA semifinals was a very talented Nevada-Las Vegas team that scored points in machine-gun fashion. The game proved to be a greyhound race, and the Tar Heels showed that their running ability was equal to that of the Runnin' Rebels. Led by O'Koren's 31 points, UNC won by a point, then faced Marquette in the championship game. It was the swan song of Marquette Coach Al McGuire, who had announced his retirement. He went out in style, his Warriors winning 67–59.

McGuire paid tribute to Smith immediately after the game, saying, "I am very sad for Dean Smith. He has such a fine club and is a great coach. I so admire the job he did in the Olympics, and he's what coaching is all about. He's a keeper, and I hope he always stays in the business."

Smith was equally gracious, saying, "I congratulate Al McGuire. It's nice to see him go out a winner, although we certainly would have liked to have won this ourselves. But I couldn't be prouder of our team even if we had won." North Carolina had overcome tremendous odds to finish 28–5. For the second straight year, the Tar Heels ended atop the ACC standings, with Smith voted conference coach of the year both seasons. His fellow coaches also selected him national coach of the year in 1977.

The decade concluded as Carolina reached the NCAA Tournament but was eliminated in the first round in both 1978 and 1979. In 1977–78, the Tar Heels placed first in the ACC regular-season standings, finishing 23–8 overall, as Phil Ford was named national college player of the year. The 1978–79 season was a year in which UNC was believed to be rebuilding, but Smith has always coached well in underdog situations. North Carolina downed eventual NCAA champ Michigan State, had an eight-game winning streak, and shared the

Phil Ford, the 1977–78 national player of the year

ACC regular-season title with Duke. The Tar Heels then upset the Blue Devils for the ACC Tournament championship. A loss to Pennsylvania in the national tourney left Carolina with a record of 23–6. Again, Smith was voted the national coach of the year, this time by *Basketball Weekly* and the Basketball Writers Association of America.

The seventies were a decade of outstanding achievement for the North Carolina basketball program, as it became recognized as a consistent national power. Carolina's coach, though he shunned the credit, was the artist of a masterpiece. This man was not just another guy named Smith.

A DECADE OF DOMINANCE

The 1980s were a marvelous decade for University of North Carolina basketball; in fact, the eighties were truly the decade of the Tar Heels in college hoops. They won 281 games, 10 more than Nevada-Las Vegas, the second winningest school from 1980–89. Most remembered, of course, is the 1981–82 Carolina team that won the national championship with a record of 32–2.

UNC dominated the tough Atlantic Coast Conference in the eighties, winning 28 more games during regular-season conference play and four more league-tournament contests than its closest challenger. The Tar Heels' average overall record in the decade was 28–6; their average in the ACC was 11–3.

Dean Smith posted a winning percentage of .817 for the eighties, .786 in the conference. He tied close friend John Thompson of Georgetown for the most NCAA Tournament victories in the decade with 25.

Smith's teams put up some big numbers in the 1980s, and

the superstars who made Carolina so powerful could form a Tar Heel Hall of Fame. Michael Jordan, James Worthy, Sam Perkins, Kenny Smith, Brad Daugherty, and J. R. Reid have gone on to become standouts in the National Basketball Association. Mike O'Koren, Al Wood, Joe Wolf, and Dave Popson also enjoyed NBA careers. Dave Colescott, Matt Doherty, Jimmy Black, Steve Hale, Jeff Lebo, and Steve Bucknall were all solid performers in the collegiate ranks.

The 1979–80 team had a senior nucleus led by Mike O'Koren and including Jeff Wolf, Dave Colescott, Rich Yonakor, and John Virgil. It also had James Worthy, a freshman loaded with potential. But Worthy went down with an injury, breaking an ankle in January. He did not return that season. Carolina finished 21–8 after tying for second place in the regular-season ACC standings. The Tar Heels were defeated by eventual champion Duke in the conference tournament semifinals. They received an opening-round bye in the NCAAs, then fell to Texas A & M in double overtime.

"I thought we'd bounce back after being beaten in the ACC Tournament," Smith said, "but our draw in the NCAA tourney was a tough one, as we had to play Texas A & M in Texas. That's why I was fighting not to have byes. It's good to get a game under your belt. It also would have been nice not to have played a Texas team in Texas. It wasn't a slouch game by any means."

The 1979–80 squad ended 15th in both the AP and UPI polls, the only time Carolina would finish out of the top 10 in the decade.

The 1980–81 Tar Heels started a streak that would continue through the eighties; nine straight UNC teams would go on to win at least 27 games. Ten straight teams would advance to the Sweet 16 of the NCAAs, a streak that is still intact.

"We had lost five seniors the year before," Smith recalled, "but fortunately, Sam Perkins arrived as a freshman even

Smith with Al Wood

more ready than we anticipated. We struggled early, going out and getting a great win in L.A. against Louisville, then losing to a very good Minnesota team [also in Los Angeles] and to Kansas at Kansas City. I think Al Wood was pressing because he wanted to have a great senior year." North Carolina finished second in the ACC standings, then edged Maryland by a point for the conference tourney championship. "We had to play Utah in Utah in the NCAAs. We beat them and then a good Kansas State team out there. We played Virginia in the national semifinals in Philadelphia, and we were really fired up for that one. Virginia had come from behind to beat us twice during the regular season." Wood was amazing against the Cavaliers, pouring in 39 points to lead UNC past Virginia 78–65.

Waiting in the championship game was Bobby Knight's Indiana team. A major distraction arose, however, as President Ronald Reagan was shot on the day between the semifinals and the finals, and for a while there was some doubt as to whether the title game would even be held. "Bob [Knight] said something about a co-championship," Smith remembered, "and that sounds nice now." But the game was played, and the Hoosiers dominated the second half on the way to a 63–50 victory. It was Smith's sixth trip to the Final Four without a title. The Tar Heels ended at 29–8, earning them a sixth-place finish in both polls.

Starters Al Wood and Mike Pepper were gone for the 1981–82 season. Their departure left a young, yet experienced, team. Worthy, a junior, had started most of the past two seasons after recovering from his ankle injury. Sam Perkins and Matt Doherty were sophomores. Perkins had been a starter the last part of his freshman season after proving himself a valuable sixth man early. Doherty had come off the bench to make a considerable contribution as a rookie. Jimmy Black was a senior, the smart, old head of the group who was in his second season as the starting point guard. And then, of course, there was Michael Jordan, a frosh, but an extraordinary frosh on his way to superstardom.

"We had no idea Michael would start coming in as a freshman," Smith said. "He wasn't the same Michael Jordan that we know today. He was a high school forward who was learning to play guard. Looking back, people let Michael shoot from outside; that's really the way it was throughout the year. He had some great moments and some not so great. But my oh my, did he ever pick up things fast! That's one of the many special things about Michael. After we had been practicing a couple of weeks, I remember our staff getting together and saying how great it was that after one of us told Michael something once, he worked at it and did it. He had been taught in high school to turn to the ball on defense when the man goes back door. We wanted him to turn and go over his

Michael Jordan

shoulder, not to open up until he hit the lane. We talked to him, showed him, and the next day, that's just the way he did it in practice. He had an amazing capacity there. He was—and is—a competitor; his work ethic was—and is—outstanding. . . .

"The guys we had coming back weren't happy to be in second place. They were more determined than ever to come back and win it. Michael joined them to give us a solid lineup.

We didn't have good depth. If we had had an injury at the end of the year like we did so many times, it would have been difficult."

As it was, Carolina just got better and better as the season progressed. Ranked number one in the preseason polls, the Tar Heels suffered their second and final loss on February 3, then won their last 16. Jordan hit some key baskets against North Carolina State to get UNC into the finals of the ACC Tournament. "In the championship game," Smith remembered, "Virginia made about every shot during a stretch in the second half. We finally said, 'Let's see if they'll come out of their zone.' That year, we weren't as good against a zone. But [Ralph] Sampson stayed under, and we had the lead. They chose not to chase. That game [a 47–45 Carolina win] had a lot to do with the shot clock being voted in. Virginia had beaten us real easily [74–58] once. It was a great victory which got us into the East Regional. We were playing [Virginia] for the home court in the NCAAs, in addition to the ACC Tournament championship."

In the Tar Heels' opening game in the national tournament, James Madison held the ball and narrowly missed a gigantic upset, falling 52–50. The Tar Heels then beat Alabama by five points and Villanova by 10. Next stop: New Orleans.

If Smith did not seem to express any passion for winning the national title in his seventh trip to the Final Four, his players did. They wanted to win for themselves, as any athletes would, but they also were making a concerted bid for their coach. "I'm tired of hearing that Coach Smith can't win the big one," Jimmy Black said on the eve of Carolina's semifinal game with Houston. "We're going to do something about it. Coach never complains, he never says anything about it, but I'm sure it hurts him because I know it hurts me. That's why we've got to win for him this time."

North Carolina defeated the Cougars 68–63, scoring the game's first 14 points, then hanging on. Houston, led by future NBA all-stars Akeem Olajuwon and Clyde Drexler, bat-

Matt Doherty protects the ball against Alabama
during the 1982 East Regional

Photo by Hugh Morton

tled back to a tie at 29 and trailed at the half by only a basket, 31–29. The Tar Heels used another fast start in the second half and their famed four-corners delay to secure the victory. Jordan sank three straight shots to keep Carolina comfortably in front, with Perkins and Doherty also scoring key hoops when Houston crept close. James Worthy's power dunk was the clincher. The Tar Heels made only three field goals in the final eight minutes and attempted just 17 the entire second half, making 13 of them for a sizzling 76.5-percent accuracy. Perkins scored 25 points and grabbed 10 rebounds for Carolina, with Jordan adding 18 points and Worthy 14.

After the win that earned UNC a championship berth opposite Georgetown and Dean Smith's friend John Thompson, the Tar Heel dressing room hardly resembled one occupied by the victors in a game of such magnitude. It was quiet, almost solemn; there were no celebrations. An unknowing visitor might have thought UNC had lost. With Smith about to embark on his fourth NCAA title-game appearance, the Tar Heels had a goal.

"We haven't won anything yet," said Matt Doherty. "Sure, getting into the finals is important, but we can't settle for that." Smith said the team's businesslike attitude was influenced by the previous year's trip to the Final Four. "We had beaten Virginia and Ralph Sampson in '81 [in the NCAA semifinals]," he recalled, "and we were so thrilled about that, you'd have thought we won the championship. Because of that, we talked and made up our minds to concentrate better. There was even a banner which said, 'Let's go one more this year.'"

The day between the NCAA semifinals and finals is supposed to be a day off for the teams. Instead, it is a media circus, with a huge throng of writers and broadcasters jamming into a hotel banquet room for press conferences and player interviews. The athletes have a short practice session in the afternoon, but the tension of the wait and the steady stream of questions are hardly relaxing.

James Worthy faces Georgetown's Ed Spriggs
during the 1982 championship game

Photo by Hugh Morton

On Sunday, the day before the Georgetown–North Carolina showdown, everyone knew Smith's lack of a championship would once again be the primary topic of discussion. His team had been ranked number one in the polls all season, and now it had to overcome a foe blessed with a wealth of talent, led by intimidating seven-foot center Patrick Ewing.

As media representatives jostled for position in order to ask their questions, Smith talked about what had been talked about so many times in the past. "A lot of coaches may feel sorry for me," he said, smiling and with tongue stuck firmly in cheek, "having been here so many times and not winning. . . . I say that jokingly. But I wouldn't trade our program. Of course, we'd like to win, but if we don't, life will still go on, we'll still have a great program, and our players will still graduate. If we don't win, I think I can handle it pretty well. My lifestyle is not one of heights and depths. We try not to have great emptiness or great ecstasy."

Years before, Smith had pointed out that others—fans and writers—made much more of his not having coached a national champion than he ever did himself. "I don't feel I've got to win a national title before I end my coaching career," he said in answer to the question of whether the absence of the big trophy on his shelf might be his one regret. "Sure, we at North Carolina would like to win one, but not just for me. We would like to win it every year, but I don't want to put too much emphasis on that. I don't think that's where the emphasis should be; I don't think that's the ultimate in coaching. I feel it's much harder to sustain a program than go all the way once. Only three coaches have been able to go to the Final Four as many as five times, whereas more than 30 have won national titles. Which is more difficult? I'm not trying to sell a championship short, but often it is a one-shot thing. There have been several times when a team was on probation just before or after winning the national championship. A team has to be very good and very, very lucky to win the title. There isn't a miniseries in which a team has to win two out of three. In college basketball, one bad night and you're out of it. A program or a career can be a success without having 'national champion' written beside a school's name."

John Thompson had his own feelings. "Dean is the most outstanding coach in the game today," he said. "All this talk about him not winning the championship . . . well, it's a lot more difficult to just get here than it is to win one ball game. Dean has been criticized for the way he does things— everything so organized—and I kid him about it. But he's done so much and still has kept things in perspective."

There was no doubt about the mutual respect Smith and Thompson shared as they prepared their teams to do battle.

The Tar Heels got ready for the title game much as they had for their 33 other contests during the season. On Sunday afternoon, they practiced, watched tapes, and discussed their opponent. Defense and rebounding were the points of emphasis, as usual. Boxing out was stressed, as always. Keeping Patrick Ewing off the boards—that was a problem in need of a solution.

Monday, game day, seemed to take an eternity to pass. Players could only eat their meals and wait. Tar Heel fans— those in New Orleans and those back in North Carolina— fretted, hoped, and recalled 1957, when UNC had last won an NCAA basketball championship. They prayed that the magic of 25 years before would be relived.

The game was a classic. Neither Carolina nor Georgetown could gain a sizable lead. Ewing goaltended five early Tar Heel shots, but the ploy did not intimidate Worthy, who went to the basket with a vengeance the entire evening. Georgetown's Hoyas owned the contest's largest advantage, six points, that coming in the first half, and they were ahead by a point, 32–31, at halftime. The lead switched hands throughout the second half, a crucial play coming after Carolina went to the four corners with over five minutes remaining: Jimmy Black drew Ewing's fourth foul, and the Tar Heel point guard made both ends of a one-and-one to give his team a three-

The 1981–82 Tar Heels take the floor

Photo by Hugh Morton

point lead. Jordan's left-handed layup over Ewing put UNC in front 61–58, and with three and a half minutes left, the three-point edge looked like breathing room. It wasn't. Ewing hit a jumper, and after Carolina's Doherty missed the front end of a one-and-one, Eric "Sleepy" Floyd sank a 12-footer for Georgetown, giving the Hoyas a 62–61 lead with less than a minute remaining and setting the stage for a bizarre ending.

North Carolina called a time-out with 32 seconds showing, and most of the 61,000 watching in the Superdome and the millions watching on national television probably figured Worthy would get the ball. Smith knew Georgetown's zone would probably prevent that, so he had other ideas. As always, he was calm in the huddle. "I honestly don't think

Coach felt the pressure," Carolina Assistant Coach Eddie Fogler said later. Smith reminded the Tar Heels that there was an abundance of time. He told them to hit the boards if their shot missed, and to foul immediately if Georgetown rebounded. It seemed likely that Georgetown would sag defensively on Worthy and Perkins to prevent either from getting an easy shot. Smith looked at Jordan just before the huddle broke and said, "Knock it in, Michael."

The call was going to a freshman. Maybe Smith had seen in his sensational rookie the same ability to come through in the crunch that would highlight a tremendous college and pro career. "We were in our zone offense with Worthy and Perkins flashing across the middle," Smith later explained. "What we wanted was to look inside, and if James was covered, to fake in there, then go across court to Michael. It was a set play."

After the Tar Heels inbounded, Black whipped a pass across the Hoyas' zone defense. Jordan showed the poise of a veteran, squaring up nicely to swish the 17-foot shot heard 'round the world. "I never even thought about missing," Jordan said later. "I had all the confidence in the world." Confidence that must have been boosted by an experienced coach's belief in a freshman player.

After what proved to be the game winner settled into the net with 17 seconds left, Georgetown had plenty of time to get a shot or two of its own. The Hoyas didn't call a time-out, choosing to head right back downcourt. Smith felt it was a smart decision, saying, "If John had taken a time-out, it would have given us a chance to set our defense." Georgetown guard Fred Brown became momentarily rattled, however, and threw the ball directly into the hands of Worthy, who dribbled to the other end of the floor before being fouled. He missed both of his free throws, but only two seconds remained, and all Georgetown could manage was a desperation heave as the buzzer sounded. The Tar Heel bench erupted. Smith and his friend John Thompson embraced at midcourt.

Sam Perkins shoots over Patrick Ewing

Photo by Hugh Morton

Worthy was named the outstanding player in the Final Four after scoring 28 points on 13-of-17 shooting, including several awesome slam dunks. A consensus all-American, he went on to be named national co-player of the year by the Helms Foundation. Jordan added 16 points and led North Carolina with nine rebounds. Perkins scored 10 points and had seven rebounds. Like Worthy, he went on to receive all-American recognition. Black handed out seven assists in addition to performing his usual quarterbacking duties. Amazingly, he did not commit a turnover against the famed Hoya press. Doherty's defense was superb.

With the NCAA title, Dean Smith completed the coach's triple crown in amateur basketball, since he had already taken teams to a National Invitation Tournament championship and an Olympic gold medal. In guiding UNC to the NCAA title, Smith joined Indiana's Bobby Knight as the only men in college basketball ever to play on a national championship team and later coach one.

Not surprisingly, Smith did not react much differently at the conclusion of the championship victory than he did after the other exciting wins his teams had pulled off over a 21-year span. He was gracious and reserved, as usual, expressing gratitude to his players and assistant coaches while praising John Thompson. "Honestly, I thought I was outcoached tonight," Smith remarked. "Fortunately, I had players who played extremely well."

The relationship between the two men left its mark on the 1982 NCAA title game. Both wanted badly to win, but both also hated to see the other lose. "It created a double problem in my mind," Thompson recalled. "It caused me to be more emotional than I normally would be . . . because of my affection for the guy sitting on the other bench. Sure, I'm disappointed that we lost, but there's no doubt in my mind that in our field, Dean Smith is one of the best—if not *the* best. A lot of what I know about coaching has come from him. In a sense,

James Worthy in action against Georgetown

Photo by Hugh Morton

I felt the student wanted to show the teacher he knew something about the game, too."

Smith had said years earlier that his life would not change drastically if his team won a championship. During postgame interviews that night in New Orleans, he conducted himself the same as always, even though the spoils of victory—mainly the championship trophy—had replaced handshakes of consolation. While Carolina fans had found barely missing the brass ring exasperating, Smith continued to place the emphasis on the consistency of the Tar Heel basketball program.

"What some people seemed to forget was that there were times when we got there—to the Final Four—that we weren't the best team, perhaps not even one of the best four teams, in college basketball," Smith noted. "But it was perceived by some that we were much better than we were. We were so happy just to be there some years. I remember one time when we were losing in the consolation game, and our fans were yelling, 'We're number four!' It was exciting for them that we had done that well. Really, there were years that we overachieved in reaching the Final Four; there were years we were simply beaten by better teams; and there were times that injuries hurt our chances. These are things that aren't always noticed or remembered when people say, 'You've gotten to the Final Four all those times, but haven't won it.' And that's why it doesn't bother me. Sure, I felt some relief when we won it, but I hadn't heard all that stuff our fans might have been hearing, and I never felt any pressure to win a national title. . . .

"I was ecstatic that we won," he said, "but I don't think it meant I was any better coach. Let's say Georgetown would have gotten the ball to Eric Floyd in the corner in the closing seconds and he would have made a shot. I don't think it would have ruined my life.

"It goes back to what you are after. Does winning that game mean you are the best team? Not necessarily. I've said it over and over—society is so caught up with that national championship, and it's not a fair way to determine a champion. Now, you play a best-of-seven series the way the pros do, and that's the best way. Basketball is a tournament sport, and that's what makes it so exciting. The championship, though, goes back to that old thing about winning the big one. How many big ones does it take to get into the finals? I was glad to win the NCAA title, but I didn't feel any pressure to do so. See, to me, there was nothing like having to win the ACC Tournament to go to the NCAAs after winning the regular-season championship. Now, that was pressure."

Reflecting on the championship itself, Smith said, "This is really the only year that it would have bothered me [not to win the NCAA title], in that I thought we had the best team this time. We were ranked number one in the country in preseason and postseason. Everybody gave us their best shot. This team had great chemistry and remarkable young men who sacrificed for the team. I am glad the game was well played, but I don't think I'm a better coach now because we've won a national championship." Of his players' determination to win for him, Smith said, "I believe in teams playing for their universities and teammates, but I was touched they felt that way about me, even though I was afraid they were putting too much pressure on themselves by trying to win for me." Smith lauded his Tar Heel reserves and made sure he mentioned Carolina players of the past, saying, "They are a part of this, too."

Kansas Coach Roy Williams, a member of the UNC staff at the time, remembers that the Tar Heel players were not the only ones badly wanting a championship for Smith. "My feeling at the end of the game was that it was such a relief . . . that now nobody could say that about Coach Smith, that he never won the . . . big one. As a staff, I think we felt it more than Coach did. We felt the pressure and heard those things more than he did because he has a great capacity to know what he's trying to do and feel good about how he's trying to do it, regardless of what everybody else says. He has some strong

The 1982 NCAA championship team—
Sam Perkins, Jimmy Black, Michael Jordan,
Matt Doherty, and James Worthy—
with announcer Billy Packer

Photo by Hugh Morton

Worthy, Jordan, Smith, Perkins, Black, and Doherty

Photo by Hugh Morton

convictions. You can criticize him or whatever, but if he still feels good about himself, that's more important."

Thousands of North Carolina students and fans descended upon the streets of Chapel Hill to toast the NCAA crown by painting the town Carolina blue. The 1982 championship party would outlast the night.

The next afternoon, under a warm March sun, over 25,000 UNC faithful provided a welcoming committee for the Tar Heels, Kenan Stadium serving as the stage for an enormous pep rally. Smith did not accompany his team, and although several reasons were given for his absence, it appeared he was simply making sure he wouldn't steal his players' thunder.

"Hey, he didn't have any other engagements," Roy Williams said. "The man made a special effort not to be there. He even told us [coaches] what his flight was and everything, and there is no doubt in my mind that the reason he did that is because he wanted the players to get the attention. He already had enough; he already had the win and the season. He did not need those other people to do things like that for him, knowing it would take away from the players."

At the Kenan Stadium celebration, Carolina players took a few moments from the festivities to talk about their coach. "So, Dean Smith can't win the big one, right?" Matt Doherty asked. "Winning the championship for Coach Smith was very important to me and the rest of the team," James Worthy said. "We were tired of hearing all that stuff that has been said about him and his teams choking in the big games. I think a lot of that man; I wanted very much to win for me and the rest of our players, but I think I wanted to win more for Coach Smith." "It sure means a lot to be on Coach Smith's first championship team," Jimmy Black remarked. "He deserved it if anyone ever has."

When the 1982 NCAA championship trophy was presented to North Carolina, the school's fans were already envisioning a repeat performance. With Black the only starter graduating, and with Worthy, Jordan, Perkins, and Doherty a year older and more experienced, the future certainly looked bright. Incoming freshmen Steve Hale, Curtis Hunter, and Brad Daugherty promised to add depth. But the bubble burst quickly. "In 1983, it was tough," Smith said. The main reason was that Worthy chose to depart, passing up his senior year of eligibility to turn pro.

"I had met in Greensboro with James and his folks," Smith said. "I had made phone calls to San Diego and Los Angeles. The only thing I do in this sort of thing is to just say to teams, 'If he's available [for the draft], will you take him?' I know the player, James in this case, is going to have to have a minimum of this certain salary, and then we lay it all out. L.A. won the flip [for the number-one pick], and the Lakers had promised to draft James if they got that first pick. But we were still nervous when it was announced . . . because we couldn't be sure until it happened. I've learned since that anything Jerry West says, you can believe. There were other factors involved besides the money. James couldn't get insurance on the ankle, and I think this was the thing that put more positives on going [pro]. . . . Also, he had played on a national champion and had a sensational year capped by a tremendous game. The financial security allowed James's dad to go back to seminary and do what he wanted to do. His mother stayed in nursing. The family didn't change. That turned out to be a very good decision, but it bothered me the next year when James wasn't in uniform. What I mean by that is that we missed him a great deal."

The 1982–83 season was filled with ups and downs. "We were a very good team," Smith noted, "because Michael came on out of nowhere. No one had him as a preseason all-America. From his freshman to his sophomore year, I've never seen such improvement. He grew an inch and a half. He worked on his game and became a true guard. His athletic ability, of course, is phenomenal, but his play as a sophomore was mostly due to his physical maturity and work habits over the summer. We would change the teams around in practice

Michael Jordan while playing with the 1984 Olympic team

Photo by Hugh Morton

scrimmages, but no matter how we did it, the team Michael played on would win.

"Most teams that have won [the NCAA title] haven't come back and done as well as we did in '83, but it was a disappointing season to our fans. It hurt to have Jordan foul out twice against N.C. State and lose both." The second loss came in the ACC Tournament semifinals, which went into overtime. North Carolina had tied Virginia for first place in the conference during the regular season. The Tar Heels defeated James Madison and Ohio State in the NCAAs before falling to Georgia in the East Regional championship game. Carolina finished the campaign at 28–8 and was ranked eighth in both major polls. Michael Jordan and Sam Perkins were consensus all-Americans, and Jordan was chosen by the *Sporting News* as the national player of the year.

The 1983–84 campaign was a fine one for UNC in many respects, and that year's team could have been the best ever at Carolina. But the season ended as one of Smith's greatest disappointments. Ranked number one in preseason, North Carolina was the favorite to capture the NCAA title. The Tar Heels won their first 21 games of the season before dropping a one-point heartbreaker to Arkansas on the road. In the 17th win, though, disaster struck in the form of an injury to spectacular freshman point guard Kenny Smith, who broke his left wrist when he was decked on a breakaway layup against Louisiana State in Chapel Hill. Smith returned to the lineup near the end of the season, but he wore a plastic cast and was not nearly as effective. Carolina won the rest of its scheduled games following the loss to Arkansas, yet some of the magic had disappeared. Though Steve Hale did an excellent job replacing Smith, the team did not have the same quickness without its rookie whirlwind. The Tar Heels seemed a bit out of step. "We just never could regain our chemistry after Kenny was hurt," Matt Doherty said. Also, Brad Daugherty injured a finger and played sparingly in the last several games.

The team sported a superb regular starting lineup that year,

Kenny Smith makes a move against
Notre Dame's David Rivers

Photo by Hugh Morton

with seniors Matt Doherty and Sam Perkins, junior Michael
Jordan, sophomore Brad Daugherty, and Kenny Smith. UNC
dominated the ACC, winning all 14 league encounters to become only the sixth team to go unbeaten in the conference's
31-year history. And the feat was accomplished in what was
perhaps the ACC's best overall season—five of the league's
eight teams played in the NCAA Tournament, with the
number-five team in the conference, Virginia, reaching the
Final Four. Duke upset the Tar Heels in the semifinals of
the ACC Tournament, then Indiana pulled the plug on what

had been a glorious season by ousting Carolina from the NCAA field in the East Regional semis.

Smith heaped praise on Bobby Knight and the Hoosiers, but it was apparent the defeat had taken a heavy toll on the Tar Heel coach. "I probably was more disappointed in the way 1984 ended than I was after any of our losses in those NCAA championship games," he said. "I thought we were the best team in '84. Anytime you can second-guess yourself, you feel worse; and I second-guessed making the change at point guard when Steve Hale was playing so well and Kenny Smith was hurt. If we had just stayed healthy . . ." Jordan was everybody's all-American and national player of the year. He was the main cog in a lineup that had size, quickness, experience, offensive punch, and defensive stability. And there was bench strength to back it up. "I thought we'd win it all," Matt Doherty said. "All of us players thought we could win it; we thought it was our year again. That makes it hurt even more." North Carolina's final record was 28–3.

Doherty and Perkins, both reliable throughout their careers, were graduating. Perkins's consistency throughout his career had made him a three-time all-American. Jordan, a junior, was also leaving, giving up his final year of eligibility to become an NBA player. The young man who grew up in Wilmington, North Carolina, had said repeatedly during his marvelous season that he was almost certain of returning to Carolina for his senior year. It was his coach who changed the superstar's mind. "We don't believe Michael's value will ever be greater," Smith explained, "plus, he could get hurt." Again, Smith demonstrated the sincerity of his interest in his players.

Jordan had been absolutely unbelievable his junior season, performing one sensational feat after another. Foul trouble seemed to be the only thing that could stop him. His dazzling dunks have become legendary, and his supremacy in all phases of basketball makes him the epitome of a complete player. The man who has frequently defied gravity departed as the best player ever produced by the ACC.

"I have Coach Smith to thank for everything," Jordan said upon announcing his decision to turn pro. "He made me a better player, he helped me improve each year, and he made me work to reach my potential. He looked into all of the possibilities involving the NBA draft, then told me he thought it was best if I went ahead and declared hardship. I am lucky to have had the chance to play for Dean Smith."

The 1984–85 Carolina team has to be considered an overachiever. For the first time since 1981, UNC was not ranked in the preseason top-20 polls. So all the Tar Heels did was tie for first place in the regular-season ACC standings and finish seventh in the final AP and UPI rankings. They won three games in the NCAAs before being ousted in the Southeast Regional by eventual national champion Villanova. UNC's final record was 27–9. Included were an impressive win at Notre Dame and a victory over Auburn in Birmingham, Alabama.

Injuries have had a way of plaguing UNC basketball teams in postseason play, and that was the case in the 1985–86 campaign. Three Tar Heel starters—Steve Hale, Joe Wolf, and Warren Martin—were hurt during the NCAA Tournament. For the second straight year, Carolina was eliminated by the team that was to win it all, as Louisville defeated the Heels in the West Regional semifinal. Senior center Brad Daugherty was an all-American choice. He established himself as the ACC's career leader in field-goal percentage, having made 62 percent of his shots over his four years. North Carolina's 28–6 record earned a final ranking of eighth in both the AP and UPI polls. But one long-running Tar Heel streak came to an end. The team finished third in the ACC regular-season standings, marking the first time in 20 years that UNC had placed lower than second. Carolina's loss to Maryland in the opening round of the ACC Tournament snapped a string of 12 years in

Brad Daugherty outstretches Virginia's Ralph Sampson

Photo by Hugh Morton

which Smith's teams had advanced at least into the semifinals of that event.

The 1986–87 season proved a magnificent one for North Carolina. Kenny Smith and Joe Wolf headed a strong senior class, Dave Popson and Curtis Hunter joining them in providing a solid nucleus. The freshman duo of J. R. Reid and Scott Williams added inside help, with sophomore Jeff Lebo and junior Ranzino Smith offering punch from the perimeter. It was a club with lots of talent and depth. The Tar Heels won 18 of their first 19 games, 16 in a row following a loss at UCLA in the season's third contest. After a defeat at Notre Dame without injured Kenny Smith, UNC won its last nine in the regular season, then made it 11 straight before being nipped 68–67 by North Carolina State in the ACC Tournament's championship battle. Carolina had gone 14–0 in the Atlantic Coast Conference, just the seventh time an undefeated league record had been accomplished. Smith's club had done it twice in four years. North Carolina scored over 100 points in two NCAA triumphs and avenged its earlier loss to Notre Dame before being ousted by Syracuse in the East Regional final. For the third time in school history and the second time under Smith, the Tar Heels won 32 games. Their 32–4 record was good for an AP final ranking of second and a third-place finish in the UPI poll. Kenny Smith was a consensus all-American selection and was named national player of the year by *Basketball Times* after setting the North Carolina career assist record.

The absence of Smith's speed left the 1987–88 Tar Heel squad with gaps that couldn't be filled. The team suffered from a lack of experience, too, with four seniors gone from the year before. Despite its weaknesses, Carolina won the ACC regular-season crown for the 15th time under Dean Smith. J. R. Reid and Scott Williams continued to mature, and their inside power was the team's strength. Jeff Lebo and Ranzino Smith helped with their long-range shooting, and Steve Bucknall emerged as a defensive standout. For the second year in a row, the ACC Tournament left the Tar Heels and their fans frustrated. UNC again reached the finals and again dropped a close one, 65–61 to Duke. Carolina won three times in the NCAAs—including a clinic-like victory over powerful Michigan—before losing to Arizona in the West Regional title game, finishing 27–7. The Associated Press ranked UNC seventh in its final poll; United Press International had the Heels eighth. Reid was a consensus all-American choice.

North Carolina entered the last season of the decade having suffered a bit of a dry spell. Since their national championship season, the Tar Heels had not won an ACC Tournament title, and there was talk that Mike Krzyzewski and his Duke Blue Devils were taking over the league. The 1988–89 UNC edition won 13 of its first 14 games in spite of playing without the injured J. R. Reid the opening nine contests. The team was an experienced one, having lost only Ranzino Smith from the previous year. Talented Rick Fox led a sophomore trio that included Pete Chilcutt and King Rice. Seniors Jeff Lebo and Steve Bucknall offered leadership. Scott Williams and Kevin Madden joined fellow junior Reid to give UNC a rugged inside attack. The club seemed to achieve a nice chemistry early. It slumped in midseason and lost its last two regular-season games, each by two points, and the outlook was not particularly bright entering the conference tournament. The ACC Tournament championship was one the Tar Heels wanted badly.

"We really went after the ACC Tournament," Smith recalled. "The regular-season winner [North Carolina State that season, with UNC tying Duke and Virginia for second place] is obviously the best team, because it has the best record over 14 games. To me, the conference tournament lost everything when it was decided more than one team from a league could go to the NCAA tourney. But the fans still think the ACC tourney is important. We hadn't won one in a while, so we really wanted to win it. We always do, but I think we wanted it a little more in '89. Since 1975, I had even given the team some time off before the conference tournament. We usually play well when we come back from a layoff, and we had taken time off before the ACC [Tournament] other years, but not in the last two. We focused like we used to when we had to win [the ACC tourney] to go to the NCAAs." The Tar Heels cruised to easy wins in the first two rounds, then won a hard-fought title game over Duke, 77–74. "I was elated to win it," Smith said. "We played hard and were intense as we had been all season. But we were disappointed because we got sent out of the East for the NCAAs. Duke beat us for the ACC championship in 1988 and stayed in the East, with us sent to the West. So, we win it in '89, but get sent out again, while Duke stays in the East. I didn't understand that."

Joining Carolina in the Southeast Regional was a hungry Michigan squad, a team the Tar Heels had eliminated from the NCAAs the two previous years. This time, Michigan prevailed in Lexington's Rupp Arena, using hot shooting to beat UNC by five points. For the fourth time in the eighties, the team that knocked the Tar Heels out of the NCAA Tournament went on to win it. Carolina finished 29–8, ranked fourth by UPI and fifth by AP. That gave UNC nine finishes in the top-10 polls in 10 years.

Smith was emotional following the season-ending loss. "I thought we could win it," he said. "Then we hit Michigan. They had not been shooting well, but they hit everything against us. We played well enough to win most games." Smith broke down during the postgame press conference, expressing his disappointment for seniors Jeff Lebo and Steve Bucknall.

It was a sad ending to a joyous decade for the North Carolina basketball program, a decade in which Dean Smith won a national championship and firmly established himself as a man whose program is a model for others around the country.

The nineties did not open in typical fashion for the Tar Heels. They took an elevator ride through the 1989–90 season, but they still managed to extend two remarkable streaks—20

Jeff Lebo

straight years with 20 or more wins and 10 successive trips to the NCAA Tournament's round of 16.

North Carolina lacked overall quickness, and its outside shooting was erratic, with junior Rick Fox the lone three-point threat of consequence. J. R. Reid had turned pro, forgoing his senior year, and his aggressiveness and production inside were missed. Scott Williams underwent an appendectomy before the season opened, and his senior season was one of inconsistency. So was the Tar Heels' campaign. When the smoke cleared, they had suffered more losses than any other Dean Smith team. As late as the first round of the NCAAs, they still had not reached the 20-win plateau.

But the club had its moments, like two wins over archrival Duke, which went to the Final Four. Carolina trounced the Blue Devils in Chapel Hill and completed the sweep by ending the regular season with a 12-point win in Cameron Indoor Stadium. In between, though, the Tar Heels could string together no more than five successive victories. They were beaten in the first round of the ACC Tournament by Virginia, an overtime loss that sent UNC reeling into the NCAA Tournament.

The team's 20th win came against Southwest Missouri State, setting up the highlight of the season. Carolina had to face Oklahoma, ranked number one in the polls, a run-and-gun outfit that put lots of points on the scoreboard. The Tar Heels jumped out to an early lead and controlled the tempo in a contest that was close from start to finish.

And what a finish it was. With the score tied and seconds remaining, North Carolina had the ball out of bounds. During a time-out, Smith drew up a play on which the outcome of the game depended. Then the Tar Heels executed that play perfectly. The inbounds pass went to Hubert Davis on the left wing. He penetrated to the middle, drawing the defense, then kicked the ball out to Fox on the right wing. Kevin Madden set a tremendous screen, allowing Fox to dribble down the right baseline to the basket. Fox sank a layup just before the buzzer

King Rice, Scott Williams,
Assistant Coach Bill Guthridge, and Smith

Photo by Hugh Morton

to give Carolina a 79–77 win. As unlikely as it seemed when the tournament pairings were announced, Smith and his Tar Heels had again advanced to the Sweet 16.

But no farther. An athletic Arkansas club used a barrage of three-pointers midway through the second half to turn a close game into a runaway and eliminate UNC in the semifinals of the Midwest Regional. The upset of Oklahoma offered some consolation, but the Tar Heels' record of 21–13 (8–6 in the ACC, which earned them a third-place tie) was disappointing nonetheless.

As the curtain dropped on the 1989–90 campaign, hopes were already high for the next season. There were five big reasons—a quintet of high school stars who made up what many followers of college basketball were calling the best recruiting class ever. Eric Montross was the last, but certainly not the least, to sign. The seven-footer waited until spring to choose the Tar Heels, after UNC had landed four prize recruits in the fall. They included high-scoring, six-ten Cliff Rozier, smooth wing player Brian Reese, point guard Derrick Phelps, and excellent shooter Patrick Sullivan.

Once again, Dean Smith had answered a challenge. Some had been saying he couldn't recruit anymore, that he couldn't go out and bring back the best blue-chippers. All he did was get five of them.

Of course, high school stars have to prove they can shine in the college arena. Yet with the combination of talented newcomers and veterans like Rick Fox, Pete Chilcutt, and George Lynch, there is promise that Smith's North Carolina basketball program will be just as exciting and successful in the nineties as it was in the eighties.

THE LITTLE THINGS

Dean Smith might fittingly be called a gentleman's general. He has become accepted as an immigrant Southern gentleman by way of Kansas, thanks to his manners, his warm smile, and his congenial personality. Still, he carries a torch of competitiveness. Sitting on the sidelines during a game, his casual air belies the fact that Smith is playing as hard as his athletes, digesting details and planning strategy. When Smith is in his element, he is in complete control; no matter what, he remains cool.

He can be rankled by an official's call. The UNC coach is considered one of the best workers of referees in college basketball, and there are more than a few opposing coaches who feel Smith's ability to apply the pressure is worth a call or two per game. Smith has not been above getting whistled for technical fouls, but he has reduced his number of T's in recent years, proving himself adept at inserting the needle gently.

The Tar Heel coach could probably have been a successful

attorney, business executive, or physician, since careful attention to detail is highly valued in those professions. Mastering the obvious is easy enough, but few take time to sort through details with equal vigor. Dean Smith does.

Smith's method of recruiting is an example of his attention to detail. Some coaches simply act as supersalesmen trying to fast-talk prestigious clients. When Smith first assumed the head-coaching position at North Carolina, recruiting was a strange creature to him. His predecessor, Frank McGuire, had depended almost solely on New York for his supply of athletes. Smith chose to shop in other locations as well— especially in North Carolina—and it did not take him long to become adept at that tremendously important facet of coaching.

Many critics—and even Tar Heel fans—bemoaned that in the late 1980s, Smith was getting beaten for blue-chip prospects, that he could no longer land the big-name player. More often than not, it was mentioned that he could not come out on top in head-to-head recruiting battles with Duke Coach Mike Krzyzewski.

As he has done so often, Smith proved his critics' assessment premature. With some saying that the Carolina coach was sliding into the background of the ACC, he set the recruiting world on its ear. For the 1990–91 season, Smith signed four players ranked among the top 15 prospects in the nation and another top-50 high school performer.

Bob Lewis, Larry Miller, Rusty Clark, Charlie Scott, Dennis Wuycik, Mitch Kupchak, Walter Davis, Phil Ford, James Worthy, Sam Perkins, Michael Jordan, Kenny Smith, Brad Daugherty, and J. R. Reid were all recruited by Smith. Clark, Scott, Davis, Ford, Worthy, Jordan, and Daugherty all grew up in North Carolina. Numerous other gems have been mined by the Tar Heel coach, who resists gimmicks and high-pressure tactics in lieu of honesty and plain talk when going after prize high school prospects. Careful planning is involved in choosing which prep phenoms will be sought by Carolina, and talent is not the lone criterion for judging athletes. Once he had reestablished the UNC program, Smith became very selective in recruiting. As many have said over the years, North Carolina never rebuilds; it simply reloads.

Smith does not use a syrupy sales pitch. "The University of North Carolina is a good selling point," he said, "so I let it sell itself. About all I can really do is tell a young man what our university has to offer, and then hope he will be interested." Over the years, Smith himself has become a strong selling point. Youngsters are well aware of former Carolina players who learned well enough under Smith to go on to stardom in the NBA. Parents know their sons are likely to receive a degree if they play for Smith.

Doing things the right way is a subject that often comes up when Smith and his Carolina basketball program are discussed. The same is true for Bobby Knight at Indiana, John Thompson at Georgetown, Krzyzewski at Duke, and Lute Olson at Arizona. Smith's reputation has to do with the fact that he does not cheat; he offers no extras in an effort to entice a talented prospect. Smith feels there is no excuse for cheating. "Any coach caught cheating should be fired," he said. "If a school is placed on probation for recruiting violations, then the coach should be fired." As for North Carolina's glossy reputation, a rival coach said, "You can go outside the Atlantic Coast Conference and ask other coaches to name three schools which are not cheating, and Carolina will always be one of the three named."

Smith's honesty in recruiting goes beyond merely abiding by the rules. Even Ford, Worthy, and Jordan were not promised an immediate place in the Tar Heel starting lineup. No one has been. "That impressed me," said Ford, who wound up one of the relatively few freshman starters at UNC. Recalling his senior year of high school, when throngs of college coaches came calling, he said, "Coach Smith didn't even promise me a spot on the varsity, much less a starting position. If he had promised I would start, well, he might have

Smith and Phil Ford

done the same thing to the guy coming in right behind me."
Smith never makes any vows except to tell prospective Tar
Heels that they will be treated like every other member of the
team and that they will be given a fair chance to play. There
have even been occasions when he was candid enough to tell
prospects that they might not see much action at UNC. "If
we're going after someone, and I don't foresee him getting a
shot at playing a lot, I'll tell him before he comes to Carolina,"
Smith said. "And I tell some they will have to work very hard
in order to play much. Everybody realizes it's tough to sit on
the bench, but we are honest." That is probably why very few
athletes shuttle in and out of the Tar Heel basketball program;
when they arrive in Chapel Hill, they normally stay four

years. Only a handful of the 177 players to earn letters under Smith have transferred to other colleges.

At the same time, players transferring from other schools are not welcomed by the Carolina coach. It is not that he has negative feelings about transfers. "No, I just don't think it's fair to the young men we've already recruited," Smith explained. "It's bad to take in a new guy and bump out one who has been here. It's a family situation, and taking a transfer is like adopting a child. It's rough on the children already in the family as well as the one who has been adopted. It's tough on him to come in after playing somewhere else and adjust to a program the others on the team already know. After our players have worked and been a part of our program, it isn't right to bring someone else from another school and play him ahead of those who have been here."

The one exception was Bob McAdoo, who came to Carolina from Vincennes Junior College, where he helped that school win a national championship while piling up sparkling statistics. "We recruited Mac because of some unusual circumstances," Smith said. "We had thought Tom McMillen was coming here the year before, but he decided at the last minute to attend Maryland. Lee Dedmon had graduated, and we needed a big man, one who could play right away. Mac's mother called me and asked why we weren't interested in her son. Also, Mac was from Greensboro, North Carolina, and we like to have players from this state. I was concerned at how things might work out with him, but everything turned out very well. Steve Previs, Bill Chamberlain, Dennis Wuycik, and Kim Huband took Mac in and made him feel welcome. I give credit to the players and to Mac; I really had no idea it would work so well."

An example of Smith's saying no to a talented transfer was guard Jim Boylan, who helped Marquette defeat the Tar Heels for the NCAA title in 1977. "He was a fine player, and we knew it," Smith said, "but we just made up our minds not to take any more transfers. So I told Al McGuire about him."

Carolina players on the sidelines

There are coaches who hit the recruiting trail every year in hopes of backing their trucks up to the high school all-American list and signing as many prospects as possible. After being accustomed to the limelight, some former prep standouts then have to take seats on the bench, and the bench can get mighty uncomfortable when its occupants are disenchanted. Smith does not risk such an overload of stars. While he does not admit to recruiting certain players for the purpose of cheerleading from the bench, Smith takes precautions not to bring in too many super talents. "We don't always go after top-10 players," he said. "There are others in whom we are interested. We obviously try to get the best athletes we can, but everyone can't start or play a lot. It takes many different types to make a team. You can have too many great players; you can overrecruit, but there is a thin line there because you still need to protect against injuries and make sure there is some depth."

Anyone who has followed basketball knows Smith has signed his share of top high school prospects, but a close look at the UNC program shows that he has also brought in numerous so-called role players.

When it is suggested that Carolina players are poured from a mold, Smith is quick to point out that he seeks athletes who possess strong character and solid academic backgrounds. "I'm too old to recruit problem types," he said. Perhaps Smith has always been too old for athletes with histories of erratic behavior. Like any other athletic team, Carolina has had players with stormy careers, but Smith's selectivity holds them to a scant few. There are no exceptions to his rigid academic standards, which are more demanding than those required by the NCAA. North Carolina players have even been suspended for a season by Smith because they fell short of his academic requirements, though they had met those of the NCAA. UNC basketball players attend classes regularly; in fact, planes are chartered for weekday road games so players can be back on campus for morning classes the following day.

Since the late 1960s, Smith's recruiting has generally guaranteed his North Carolina teams good depth. At times, there has been quality talent blessing the Tar Heel bench, but on other occasions, the pickings have been a bit sparse. Regardless of their talent level, Carolina reserves have consistently been key figures in the team's success. One of the reasons has been Smith's assignment of well-defined roles to all of his players. It also helps that he relies on his bench without regard to the game situation, showing confidence in his reserves and thereby helping them build confidence in themselves.

"We establish roles just before the season begins," Smith

said. "I want our players to know where they stand. This is important. If they are reserves and if they know who they replace, they can be ready. I have learned if each player knows how much playing time he can expect, he will play more relaxed. Security relaxes players." Tar Heel players are instructed to give their best effort for as long as they can, then give Smith the tired signal by raising a clenched fist. Tar Heel reserves know which starters they may replace. "I remember in the NCAA semifinals in 1977, when we were playing Nevada-Las Vegas," Smith said. "Walter Davis gave the tired sign, and by the time I looked down the bench, there was Dudley Bradley already taking off his warmups. He knew to go in for Walter. He knew what his role was."

Smith has usually stuck with a set starting lineup, but he has used other methods of distributing playing time as well. In 1988–89, for example, the composition of the starting five changed with almost every game, Smith rewarding the top five defensive performers from the previous contest with a chance to start. The Tar Heel coach has never believed that starting lineups should hold special significance. "It's which five players finish a game that is important, not which five start it," he maintains. There are usually eight Tar Heels who are used extensively once a rotation is established.

In the seventies, the Blue Team, a unit made up of five players who normally saw little action, was a popular part of North Carolina basketball. Smith remembered the group's conception this way: "I was disgusted with the way our starters were playing, so I told the bench I wanted five hustlers to go in. I got the idea from watching Duster Thomas's team at Pinkneyville High School in Illinois. He used to send in a new team in the second quarter, and it would press all over the court." UNC's Blue Team would enter the game in the first half and play about two minutes, applying constant pressure on defense and whipping the ball around on offense to keep the opposition moving. The group was extremely effective during the decade, taking great pride in building upon leads inherited from the starters or, at worst, not losing any ground. The Blue Team accomplished several important functions. It provided the starting team a breather. It allowed five bench players to feel very much a part of Carolina's scheme of things. And it made Blue Team members more relaxed if they were needed at a crucial time in the second half, since they had already been on the floor. Another reason for using the Blue Team was that the opposition, seeing a huge mismatch, often became overanxious because it felt the going would be easy. In the eighties, Smith began to feel that the concept had lost its impact, and he discontinued its use.

North Carolina's Tar Heels under Smith have typified teamwork both on and off the court. Smith perceives a college athletic team to be much like a family unit. One of the reasons for Carolina's closeness is that Smith allows Tar Heel seniors to sit down with him and establish rules for the squad that serve as guidelines for players' deportment away from the hardwood. "This works well," Smith said, "and the main reason we do this is to help remind our young men to be fair to each other. Also, a coach must be fair to his players. And then, I have to remember what I have done before in the area of punishment for specific actions. Say a player is one minute late for practice. That minute is valuable. I'll ask the seniors what I did for the same infraction in past years. That way, I don't let one player off lighter or make it tougher."

Smith's contempt for tardiness—whether for team meals or practice sessions—is something his players learn quickly upon their arrival in Chapel Hill. "It is an unselfish act," he said of being on time. "When someone is late, it's like saying he only cares about his own time, not that of the other people involved. Certainly, there are times when it can't be helped. I have excused it happening when players had labs or things like that. But good planning will prevent people from being late most of the time. If we care about others and value their time, it won't happen often."

Unselfishness is as characteristic of Tar Heel basketball as

Mike O'Koren passes against a tough Duke defense

the team's trademark blue-and-white uniforms. It might even be said that assists are more in vogue than points for Smith-coached Carolina teams. An uncontested 15-foot jumper is considered a high-percentage shot, yet the Tar Heels revel in passing up 15-footers for 12-footers, 12-footers for eight-footers, and eight-footers for layups. Carolina players work hard to set screens to free teammates in close, and they look for the open man rather than the open shot. It is no accident that the Tar Heels are consistently among the nation's leaders in field-goal percentage.

"We have excellent players at Carolina," Smith said. "They enjoy helping someone else score. In basketball, participants certainly learn the value of someone else helping, and then the value of saying thank you. When your team gets the ball, a player needs a teammate to take the ball out of bounds; right away, you need help. No one can do it by himself." At UNC, the offspring of this dependency is the acknowledgment of a teammate's pass by a player who makes a basket; Carolina scorers can be seen pointing to the teammates who made the assists. "John Wooden's teams at UCLA and my dad's high school teams both acknowledged the good pass, maybe with a wink or something. We made it an outward acknowledgment, pointing, because I just wanted the fans to know when a nice pass had been made. More and more teams are doing it now," Smith said.

Phil Ford is Carolina's all-time leading point maker. Still, the jackrabbit guard averaged 20 points only in his senior year. He delighted more in handing out passes than in swishing one of his patented jump shots. There have been dozens of Tar Heels who possessed the tools to be prolific scorers during Smith's 29 years as Carolina's head coach, but only Billy Cunningham, Bob Lewis, and Charlie Scott averaged as many as 25 points for a season. In Smith's first five years at the helm, Cunningham did it twice (26.0 in 1963–64 and 25.4 in 1964–65) and Lewis once (27.4 in 1965–66). Scott had his highest-scoring season (27.1 in 1969–70) the year after Rusty

Clark, Dick Grubar, and Bill Bunting graduated. Cunningham, Lewis, and Scott shot and scored more often than other players under Smith because they had to; they were not blessed with strong supporting casts. In fact, no Tar Heel team featuring a highly prolific scorer has been able to win 20 games in a season. When given the opportunity to blend into a more talented unit, Lewis and Scott scored less for Carolina teams that won more. Billy C never had such an opportunity; he had to be the whole show.

Almost every season, there is a Carolina sharpshooter of whom it is said, "If he played for another team, he could average 30 points." John Wooden at UCLA and Al McGuire at Marquette won NCAA titles with the same theory of offensive balance Smith subscribes to at UNC. While there may be nights when a player can light up the scoreboard frequently enough to produce a victory almost single-handedly, there will likely be a greater number of nights when the team will lose if that same player suffers a poor game.

Tar Heel teamwork goes deeper than a simple willingness to pass the basketball. There is a unity on Smith's squads that has a distinct family air. It is seen in the way an outstanding Tar Heel effort is applauded by the Carolina bench. It is also seen in the way rookie players are taught to be humble. First-year Tar Heels carry tape players and other items on road trips. This may be considered a task for the managers on most teams, but freshmen, with or without star billing, shoulder the burden at North Carolina. They also chase all the loose balls at practice.

Practices are special times for Smith, who loves the teaching aspect of his profession more than any other. Every minute is put to good use. Practice always starts right on time, and there is a schedule of drills that does not vary. Practices are almost sacred to the Carolina coach, who has missed only a handful of his teams' workouts—for funerals and illnesses—over the course of 29 years. The only acceptable reasons that players may miss practice are injury, home emergency, or

Smith during a Tar Heel practice

Photo by Hugh Morton

study. Smith has never accepted telephone calls during practice sessions. "I also have refused to talk with anyone during practice time," Smith said, "and this would include alumni, the chancellor, or the athletic director. There are 22 other hours in the day when I can be reached."

The six-week preseason practice period is called "boot camp" by former Tar Heels. Workouts are planned well in advance of the October 15 starting date, with master, weekly, and daily practice plans. When Smith sounds a whistle to signal the start of practice, Tar Heel players sprint to the center of the court. The team spends a few minutes there as the UNC coach cites a thought for the day and an emphasis of the day, one dealing with offense and the other with defense. Practices usually last two hours during preseason and an hour and a half during the season. Student managers write down everything that happens during practice; in fact, they record everything each North Carolina player does in practices and games. A plus-points system allows players to be recognized for dishing out assists, taking charges, grabbing loose balls, and performing other fundamentals the program stresses. The head manager keeps up with plus points, which are used by players to reduce wind sprints after practices. Plus points can even be carried over from one season to the next.

Neither players nor coaches kneel or sit during practices. Pauses are rare, with Smith and his assistants taking UNC players from one drill to the next according to schedule. Four corners and other late-game situations are practiced throughout the season, so that good habits are formed for game conditions. Wind sprints conclude each practice even during the season, as Smith has noted that "there is much to gain from being pushed to work harder. This kind of effort builds mental toughness." Each player is assigned a time when he is expected to run sprints. Everything in practice from start to finish is handled in a calm, businesslike manner. The work ethic, good habits, and practiced poise all carry over into games.

Michael Jordan and Sam Perkins
with Smith during a practice session

Smith reciprocates his players' efforts in practice by being a
confidant, an adviser, and a friend. "Our players, the ones we
have in school right now, are my first priority," Smith said. "I
mean, if the governor calls while I have one of our players in
my office, then the player has to come first; the governor will
have to wait. Some people, if they were sitting with the governor, wouldn't take a call from anybody. Well, we try to say
the most important people are the people in our program at
the present time. Next come our former players, and if one of
them phones, our secretaries are told to put the call through
even though someone with an appointment is sitting in my
office."

Much fuss has been made over Smith's habit of handwriting letters to all his former players, their number now nearing 200. But the Tar Heel coach shrugs it off, saying, "If you really like them, you want to keep the relationship with your players. Once a young man plays in this program, he is part of a larger family. . . . A person stays in touch with his family; and when you say our team is like a family, why wouldn't I want to stay in touch with players by writing?" Smith lends aid to players who have graduated, helping them find jobs or hook on with pro teams. He also counsels them with their problems. "It's normally a case of us becoming better friends after the players get out of school," Smith said. "We have practically lived together four years, and I'm bound to be concerned about them and their futures. The players spend a lot of time during their college careers helping us coaches, and the way I look at it, it's a two-way street."

Smith illustrated how athletes' willingness to give of themselves can inspire their coaches. "It was a late September night," he said, "and Mike O'Koren and Dudley Bradley were out running. Now, this is not a normal thing to be doing late at night, and, I might add, without being told to. Eddie Fogler [then a Carolina assistant coach] saw Mike and Dudley, but they didn't see him; they weren't doing this to be seen. They were just out there running, running up a hill, to get in shape for the season. It's hard to punish yourself like that. So all of our coaches feel we can give some of our time to the players. That's what I try to do. . . .

"I think that anytime a person does something hard, something which is difficult, there is a camaraderie which comes with the experience which is hard to achieve other places," Smith said. "For instance, the players coming out on the court and running sprints or doing anything they really don't want to do. I think whenever a coach and his former players get together and say, 'Hey, remember the day we did this and that,' it's always the hard things, like some of our defensive drills, which are talked about."

A Carolina victory celebration

Smith's willingness to spend time with players is at least partially attributable to his father's relationship with members of his Kansas high school teams, as well as to Smith's own experience with a former coach after graduating from Kansas University. "I remember during the war," Smith said, "when Dad's ex-players came home on furlough. They would always come over and talk with Dad, and that was impressive to me. . . . I think most coaches have great regard for their players, and I saw that firsthand. I know Dad used to have his players over to the house. At high school reunions, some people may go back and pick out an English teacher to visit, but most males have gone back to see their coaches. Dad had that kind of relationship with his athletes. Then I could see what a great interest Dick Harp was taking in the young men's lives there at Kansas. He would still call me or write me when I was at Air Force, and I appreciated that."

Mutual respect is the key to player-coach relationships as far as Smith is concerned. "The player and coach have to respect one another," he said. "They don't necessarily have to like each other, but there must be respect. Then there has to be mutual confidence. I like our players to have confidence in what I'm telling them to do and I like to show confidence in all our players. I want to take a genuine interest in a player's personal life—not a passing interest, but a sincere interest. Also, I can't say my door is always open and then never open it. I want to have time for my players. I enjoy watching our players grow while they are at the University of North Carolina. It's fun seeing that growth take place. But I don't in any way want to take credit for the maturity which may take place; the parents have done the job before the athlete gets here. And it is important that we communicate adult to adult, with me still being the boss on the court. Those things make a solid player-coach relationship, I think."

Smith's respect for his players is reflected in the fair treatment he gives them. No Tar Heel has to dread a tongue-lashing from his coach after a costly or careless error during a game. Smith approaches players with restraint rather than red-faced tirades. "If a guy throws a ball away," Smith said, "I tell him, 'Heck, I threw one away once myself.' The important thing is he's trying. And that's why we stand and cheer as a team—because this player is out there for all of us. If I get on a player, it will be with the player and me in my office; nobody else is going to know about it. . . . The players get our wins, and I get the losses. That's the way it's got to be if they're going to do what I ask them; I mean, that's the only way. You'll never hear me say anything about a player's performance determining the outcome of a game we lose. . . .

"But I do get angry," Smith said. "Sometimes, at practice, players don't do what I think they should, and I get upset.

Yes, I really get angry. I run 'em out of practice. When this happens, a player leaves practice and has to see me before coming back." So Bobby Knight is not the only coach to have sent a player to the showers early.

Never does a group of players and coaches go through an entire season without differences of opinion. Smith doesn't hold grudges. In fact, he often goes out of his way to make sure players understand what he's trying to do. Former UNC all-American Dennis Wuycik remembers an incident from the eve of his final college game. "We went to Los Angeles [for the 1972 Final Four] with everybody expecting us to play UCLA in the finals," Wuycik said. "Florida State upset us, and so we had to play a consolation game, something nobody really wanted to play, but which was still being held in those days. We were having a little shoot-around the day between games, and afterwards, we sat around and talked about where everybody was going. Coach asked who was going back with the team and who would be flying back on their own. Bill Chamberlain said he was going back on his own. Coach said, 'Okay, Bill, that's fine; you're a big boy.' Bill got all upset and said, 'Don't call me boy.' He was taking it as a racial insult. No one else thought anything about it, and Coach sure didn't mean it that way. He even said, 'Bill, I think of all my players as my boys.'

"I was rooming with Bill," Wuycik recalled, "and that night, I was standing near the elevator, talking with my dad. Coach got out of the elevator and asked if Bill was in the room. I said he was, and Coach asked if he could have a few minutes. He went in, and they must have talked for almost an hour."

Smith remembers that he was not happy at the time. "No, I was angry with Bill," he said. "I went back up there to make sure he understood how I felt. I told him he didn't have to play in that last game. Today, we're friends. That was a long time ago."

The esteem in which Smith holds all of his players, stars and second-stringers alike, is illustrated by the case of Randy

Wiel, now a member of the UNC coaching staff. Wiel was a reserve who was used sparingly before he graduated in 1979. A native of Curaçao, Netherlands Antilles, he was 28 years of age when he finished at North Carolina. Strong and muscular, he was called the Tar Heels' best all-around athlete by Smith. Following Wiel's senior season, the Carolina coach explained how a substitute could make a valuable contribution even if his minutes on the basketball court were few. "No one will ever think we're going to miss Randy next season," Smith said, "but we will. He was always talking it up on the bench and was a great leader. He was a great example of a young man accepting his role. No one likes sitting on the bench; I'm sure Randy didn't, but he had the maturity to accept it. It's people like him who help make a team close."

In Dean Smith's view, little things loom large in putting together a basketball team. His efforts are designed to ease the travail of a sport filled with tumult and pressure. It's no wonder that the Tar Heels have been so prosperous on the court for almost three decades, and that they have had so much fun doing it.

THE SMITH BLUEPRINT

Dean Smith has sketched the ideal blueprint for a winning basketball program. His North Carolina teams possess all the qualities necessary for a sturdy structure, beginning with a strong foundation and materials of the highest grade.

Although he has sorted through every particle of basketball wisdom available, rubbed psyches with some of the game's most accomplished coaches, and studied the intricacies of roundball with diligence, Smith has always been an originator. Still, he admits to being a part of all he has encountered. He has learned much from other coaches, and his own ideas have been affected by the views and methods of others. All this has combined to form a sound basketball philosophy.

"Dr. Phog Allen, Dick Harp, and my dad were the most influential people in my early philosophy on basketball," Smith recalled. "And then, later, Bob Spear and Frank McGuire had a great deal of input. At first, I thought there was only one way to do things, and that was the way Dick

Harp and Doc Allen had taught me. Doc was fundamentally strong, and Dick came up with our half-court pressure defense, which was totally new at the time. He taught playing between the man you were guarding and the ball, whereas the old books on basketball said to stay between the man and the basket. Obviously, Bob Spear was the greatest teacher I worked with, and he had to be. He had to be so patient with the players we had at the Air Force Academy because they weren't overly talented and we had a six-four height limit. Bob was such a patient teacher, and he approached his job with confidence. Also, while I was at the academy, I went to a couple of Henry Iba's clinics, and that was a tremendous experience. When I came to Carolina, there was Frank McGuire, and he was a brilliant leader."

Not surprisingly, portions of Smith's philosophy were formulated to counter techniques he didn't think worked well in other coaches' systems. A prime example is the Tar Heel coach's practice of resting his players liberally, even at their own request. "When I was playing at Kansas," Smith said, "Dr. Allen believed that a player should be in shape and therefore should play the whole game. Dean Naismith, our trainer, would watch us, and if someone looked like he was dying out there on the court, Dean would get him out. But then Dr. Allen would forget about that player, and he could never get back into the game. So no one ever said anything about being tired. Because of that, my first rule when I became a head coach was this: you bust your tail out there, then the minute you're hurting the team, you let me know by giving the tired signal, and then tell me when you can go back in. The player actually puts himself back in by telling me he's ready. See, if we had ever said to Dean Naismith we were tired, Dr. Allen would have forgotten all about us; no player wanted anybody to know he was tired. Of course, I didn't play so much that I was ever tired, but there were times out there I thought I was going to die. I decided then that if I ever coached, my team was going to have a tired signal."

Division I Men's All-Time Wins Through 1990

Years in Division I Only

	School Name	First Year	Yrs.	Won	Lost	Tied	Pct.
1.	Kentucky	1903	87	1,479	489	1	.752
1.	North Carolina	1911	80	1,479	544	0	.731
3.	Kansas	1899	92	1,432	669	0	.682
4.	St. John's	1908	83	1,421	604	0	.702
5.	Oregon State	1902	89	1,373	844	0	.619
6.	Duke	1906	85	1,345	686	0	.662
7.	Temple	1895	94	1,332	725	0	.648
8.	Notre Dame	1898	85	1,323	648	1	.671
9.	Pennsylvania	1902	89	1,315	753	0	.636
10.	Syracuse	1901	89	1,292	619	0	.676
11.	Washington	1896	88	1,279	776	0	.622
12.	Indiana	1901	90	1,242	695	0	.641
13.	Western Kentucky	1915	71	1,223	574	0	.681
14.	UCLA	1920	71	1,221	552	0	.689
15.	Princeton	1901	90	1,218	790	0	.607
16.	Fordham	1903	87	1,217	869	0	.583
17.	North Carolina State	1913	78	1,214	652	0	.651
18.	Bradley	1903	86	1,210	719	0	.627
19.	West Virginia	1904	81	1,208	724	0	.625
20.	Purdue	1897	92	1,204	683	0	.638
21.	Illinois	1906	85	1,192	652	0	.646
22.	Washington State	1902	89	1,179	1,056	0	.528
23.	Louisville	1912	76	1,174	618	0	.655
24.	Utah	1909	82	1,170	675	0	.634
25.	Texas	1906	84	1,157	748	0	.607
25.	Montana State	1902	88	1,157	879	0	.568

Information courtesy of NCAA

Smith and the Carolina bench

Far more often, other coaches' influence was positive, as is reflected in Smith's efforts to instill confidence, but not cockiness, in his players. "I would say it is our philosophy at Carolina to play with confidence," Smith said. "We want the players to feel good about themselves, and we do anything we can as coaches to help them feel that way. Now, that doesn't mean we don't criticize. We do criticize in practice. I still do not have the bad habit of swearing, but I will yell at the players. I think you can do that without profanity. Frank McGuire was a great one for instilling confidence. I remember a great way he had of telling his team how to handle a pressing defense. He said to the players, 'I'm not going to diagram how you're going to get the ball upcourt. What do you think I recruited you for? I knew you could get it up the court.' Frank was one of the best I've ever seen, perhaps the best, at making a player think he could handle any situation. I think he was amazing at that. He made me think I was the best assistant coach who ever lived; he even gave the secretary a feeling of confidence. He had a unique way."

So does Smith, taking careful steps to ensure that his Tar Heels believe in themselves and each other. Negativism has no place in his system; criticism is always constructive.

On the court, the Tar Heels function completely within the team concept their coach loves and strongly believes in. Simply put, he sees teamwork as the best road to victory. "We believe in an unselfish game," he said, "but one which is also fun for the players."

Smith's background in Phog Allen's disciplined freelance attack was supplemented by his knowledge of the passing game Henry Iba used at Oklahoma State. In Carolina's passing game, everyone moves without the ball. "We started our passing game back in 1966," Smith said, "and it has been very effective for us. . . . It has been our offense from the late sixties up until today, but it probably became most famous when Indiana used it in '75 and '76, winning the national title in '76."

It was Indiana Coach Bobby Knight who started calling the passing game a motion offense. "Bobby came down here, and we talked about the passing game," Smith said. "He told me he wanted to try it, and I remember Bobby saying, 'I don't know if we'll use it that much.' Then he called in November of the following season and sent me practice films of his team, and that's all they were doing on offense. But they were setting screens away from the ball better than we had.

"We take more or less the freelance approach to the passing game, in that we try to stay away from too many rules. We're trying to score points like everyone else, and we like to have flexibility. We rely mostly on our man-to-man offense, but when you have very good players, you tend to see more zone defenses. We believe in the fast break and always have; the transition game has been very successful for us, and it still is. But people are getting better about getting back on defense. I like to get the ball down quickly and attack before the opposition's defense is set."

When Smith assumed the head-coaching position at North Carolina, he felt his limited personnel could be utilized most efficiently through a set offense with numerous options. Tar Heel players were encouraged to improvise on a set play if there was good reason to do so. But despite the urging, Carolina coaches noted in game films that the Tar Heels sometimes missed easy scoring opportunities as a result of being too intent on executing set plays. That fact sent Smith and his staff in search of an offense that would keep the players' minds from becoming so cluttered that they could not concentrate on playing basketball. At that same time, Carolina was using a freelance zone offense with a high-low post and employing some of the principles used by Henry Iba's 1964 United States Olympic team. Larry Brown had played on that team, and as Smith's assistant coach at Carolina, he was able to incorporate some of Iba's principles into the offense already being utilized by the Tar Heels.

The result was an attack suitable for use against man-to-man defenses, but with the same freedom the zone offense had allowed. More movement and screens were added, and ultimately the freelance passing game for which Smith and the Tar Heels have become so well known was born.

Smith pointed out the advantages of the passing game. "It is a simple offense to learn," he said, "and that is an obvious advantage. This allows us to introduce it fully during the first day of practice, thus providing the offense with an organized approach when it comes time for us to work on team defense. The variety of situations created by the passing game makes defensive practice more meaningful. Exposure to the passing game helps enhance many of the skills required for efficient execution of our set game. It improves the ability to read or recognize defenses. It helps players move better without the ball. Also, players become less mechanical in their overall movements and more fluid in execution of the set game. The versatility of the passing game allows it to be used with equal effectiveness against any defense. It permits the players the freedom to hunt the open spots without being tied to thinking of specific patterns. The players seem to enjoy the chance to think for themselves in these situations. It helps their confidence and increases their ingenuity."

Another offense Smith has installed at North Carolina is the "T" game, which places a premium on pitching the ball to tall players positioned close to the basket. Like the freelance passing game, the "T" game may be used against man-to-man and zone defenses. It was first employed at Chapel Hill by the 1965–66 freshman team, which included six-foot-ten-and-a-half Rusty Clark. "We were looking for some sort of inside-oriented offense," Smith said, "since for the first time in my tenure as head coach we were blessed with a natural post man. Rusty was an outstanding passer and shooter. We needed an offense to make use of his strengths; but since he was not exceptionally quick, we wanted this offense geared to keep him within 15 feet of the basket." Combining Kansas Coach Ted Owens's use of the single-post offense and Kansas State's use of the lob pass when the post defense was playing in front of the center, Smith came up with the "T" game. It developed as a single-post offense with adjustments to best utilize the Tar Heels' personnel. Lately, it has been used only against zones.

"It is first designed as an inside attack," Smith said of the "T" game. "It lends itself to the high-percentage shot and a greater opportunity to place the opposing team in foul trouble. We try to establish our inside game; and when the defense adjusts, easy outside shots and good rebounding position become more readily available. Offensive rebounding is another advantage of this offense, because the bigger players, the forwards and centers, are never too far from the basket. Their rebounding paths are patterned to provide a strong offensive-rebounding triangle. Continuity is a feature of the 'T' game, in that it gives a team the opportunity to control the ball in an organized manner while working for the good shot. Flexibility is provided, since adjustments may be made from one year to the next to suit personnel. It can be used as a single-, double-, and triple-post offense."

Carolina is capable of striking swiftly with its fast break. The Tar Heels can also set up offensively and force the ball close to the basket, and they can hit the offensive boards. But the most famous—or infamous, according to some coaches—of all the Carolina offensive ploys was probably the four corners. Perhaps it was the success the Tar Heel delay game enjoyed that made it such a source of aggravation to the opposition. Very few times did Carolina carry a lead into four corners and lose a game. Over 80 percent of the leads UNC owned when going into four corners were increased with the delay in operation.

Such facts were no solace to Tar Heel foes and their followers prior to the shot clock's introduction into college basketball. A chorus of boos often descended upon Carolina when it went to four corners during road games, and opposing coaches were usually beside themselves with frustration after a narrow loss to the Tar Heels was sealed by the spread offense. It was a near-perfect delay game.

Smith explained the evolution of the four corners, saying, "During my first two years as head coach at North Carolina, we had the need to make extensive use of a delay game. Our delay against man-to-man defenses involved our standard offense with options, while our delay against a half-court zone press had us passing the ball around four corners, using our best ball handler in the middle. Many teams used the four corners against a zone press, although most of those teams placed their big man in the middle. Our change to just one delay game came late in the 1963 season and resulted from a fluke occurrence during a practice while we were working on our zone-press delay.

Phil Ford, master of the four corners

"Larry Brown was doing his usual fine job as the chaser in the middle," Smith said, "and the defense was having no success getting the ball. I called the defense together, suggesting they begin in a zone press and then switch to a man-to-man press. I was looking for Larry to spot the switch and move the offense into our man-to-man delay. He missed the change, however, and simply drove around his man to the goal and passed off to our center, who was left open when his man came out to stop Larry. . . . Most defenses which are behind late in a game will generally line up man-to-man and then double-team the dribbler. That one simple play in practice made it suddenly clear that we could use our zone delay equally well to spread man-to-man coverage, thereby allowing us to operate one-on-one. We were further encouraged in this direction by observing Chuck Noe, the outstanding South Carolina coach at the time, who used his 'Mongoose' as an effective man-to-man delay. The Mongoose had three men stationed across the 10-second line and two men playing two-on-two inside."

The Tar Heels did not go to four corners as their only delay game until 1966, and the ploy became an overwhelming success. Smith felt the four corners received too much attention, his main complaint being that critics labeled the Tar Heel offense a freeze. "It really was an offense which consumed time while drawing the opposition into defensive errors, resulting in a score or a foul shot," he explained. Smith's teams have answered the criticism that they play at a slow pace by remaining among the highest-scoring teams in the college game over the past 20-plus years.

Smith summed up his offensive philosophy by saying, "We first of all make adjustments in our basic system every year in order to make the most of our personnel. We don't necessarily try to do something with one group which we did with another, because the players and their talents might call for something else. So we keep an open mind. We always encourage team play, and we achieve results through cooperation and unselfish effort on the part of every player. At North Carolina, we place a man's scoring average in what we consider to be its proper perspective.

"We look to fast-break at every opportunity and always concentrate on the high-percentage shot with good offensive-rebounding coverage. We have always been dedicated to the running game; we try to fast-break on every pass we intercept as well as every missed field-goal attempt by the opponent. If a high-percentage shot is not available out of the break or secondary break, the offense automatically swings into the passing game.

"By having the team thoroughly prepared to face all possible defenses, we try to eliminate the element of surprise," Smith said. "We'll try to vary our offense during the course of a game to prevent the opposing defense from preparing too easily or becoming accustomed to one style. We use a multiple offense with major emphasis on a freelance offense with rules, along with some set offenses to make use of our personnel."

As varied and inventive as North Carolina's offense is, the Tar Heels' defense has been the most distinguishable mark etched by Smith. Carolina utilizes a multitude of defensive alignments, constantly switching among them. Because of its complexities, Carolina's defensive system is not easy to learn. More than one sweet-shooting rookie has required a lengthy period to earn extensive playing time because he could not master the Tar Heel defense. But not many opponents master it, either.

"Defensively, I believe in doing things to keep the other team from doing what it would like," Smith said, explaining his maze of man-to-man, zone, trap, and pressure defenses. "If there is something a team has practiced to use against us, we want to take the other team out of that. We don't want the other team to take advantage of all those hours of practice. Many defenses are predicated on reacting to the action initiated by the offense. Our aim is to initiate the action on de-

Bobby Jones, one of Carolina's all-time great defenders

fense and force the offense to react to us. By keeping our opponents busy trying to work their way out of our defensive attack, we hope to prevent them from doing what they want to do and generally do best. Since change necessitates more reaction than something constant, we find one of the best ways to keep the offense reacting is through a multiple defense. We strive to get the other team away from what it had planned to do offensively and make it do something different. We want to catch the opponent off guard. I'm not saying we always accomplish all these things, but those are our goals defensively.

"We do gamble a lot defensively, and we like to think everything we do is done in an attacking manner. We play up on the ball and put good pressure on the ball. Once in a while, we come back with a zone; but even then, I hope we'll be aggressive in it. We prefer man-to-man, but if we're in foul trouble or if we're ahead with three minutes to go in a game, the use of a zone is dictated. If a team sees a zone, it often ends up shooting outside against you, and then your chances of getting the rebound are pretty good. I think our players enjoy playing defense; they know they have to. I think defense is a vastly underrated part of basketball. It helps our offense, too. We led the nation in field-goal percentage over a 10-year period, and although we're unselfish and take good shots, a big reason for our shooting accuracy is because we steal the ball so frequently. We then go down and get layups off the break, so our defense really enhances our offense."

Carolina players work hard on defense. "Our players really take pride in defense here," Smith said. "If they go on and get to the NBA, they may have to change their philosophy of defense. But the whole point is that they will have learned to play defense our way while understanding the basic principle behind it. I think our players are fundamentally sound defensively. I didn't think our defenses would go in the pros until Larry Brown tried them with the Carolina Cougars. I thought the skill level would be too great; but amazingly enough, Lar-

Larry Brown, coach of the San Antonio Spurs

ry said he would run-and-jump someone or double-team somebody, and they would want to make a great pass, and consequently would throw the ball away sometimes. So Larry felt our defensive philosophy was effective even at the pro level."

The run-and-jump is the most renowned of Smith's defensive innovations, but it is also the most misunderstood. "That's terrible terminology," the Tar Heel coach said. "It probably should be called leave-and-surprise or run-and-surprise, because that's just what happens. One defensive player leaves the man he is guarding and runs over to surprise the dribbler by trying to steal the ball. I got the idea from Al Kelley, who played at Kansas when I did. Al was so aggressive that he actually would leave his man and run over to try and steal the ball from someone else's man who was dribbling. It was just freelance then, with the other guy on our team running over to pick up Al's man. We'd say, 'There goes Al, doing it again.' Al was very good at doing this. . . . Several of us on the team decided it would be fun to surprise the dribbler. This was part of our basic man-to-man pressure defense and was not used as a separate defense at that time. This is how the run-and-jump began."

Today, Smith uses the run-and-jump differently from the way he did in his early days. "When I first became head coach at the University of North Carolina, we were very small," he said, "but [we] did have three very quick guards in Larry Brown, Donnie Walsh, and Yogi Poteet. They executed the run-and-jump well, and we encouraged our forwards to enter into it anytime a dribbler approached them. Our players enjoyed the run-and-jump so much during that time, it eventually created a problem for us. Although it was not yet a separate defense, our players were given the freedom to use it at any point on the court they felt they could surprise an approaching dribbler. But surprise is important to the run-and-jump, and its effectiveness tends to diminish when it is used too often. We finally had to do something to cut down on its frequency and did this in 1965 by making it a separate, signaled defense."

Smith emphasized that the main purpose of the run-and-jump is to show the opposing offense a different look. "Our secondary defenses in our multiple-defense system are used primarily to support our basic man-to-man pressure attack. When they do work well for us, it is usually because our opponents are more disconcerted by the change than necessarily overcome by their quality or execution.

"But our run-and-jump does offer other advantages in addition to offering another look. It is not passive, but definitely initiates the action on defense. Therefore, when successful, it tends to prevent opponents from organizing their planned attack. When a defensive man leaves the man he is guarding and surprises the dribbler, it is going to result in some kind of reaction on the part of the offense. The ball handler then might charge the defender, walk with the ball, or lose it on a steal. If we succeed in making the ball handler stop his dribble, we would then try to press him and cut off his passing outlets. If we do not prevent the pass, we may still be able to offset offensive organization by forcing the ball handler into a pass he didn't intend to make. The run-and-jump usually gets things going, and for this reason, it can be used to speed up the tempo against teams which like to control the ball. We also use the run-and-jump in order to make the other team's best shooter give up the ball. We try to keep him from getting it back, and although someone else may get a good shot, at least we have made someone else shoot instead of the star player. The run-and-jump is effective against teams which like to set screens for the dribbler at the point of the ball because the man guarding the screener can approach the dribbler. As a catch-up defense . . . the run-and-jump is good to use because it is aggressive and maximizes the chance for a mistake by the other team."

The run-and-jump is just one of Carolina's many defensive strategies. Smith's Tar Heels present a vast repertoire of

Joe Wolf on defense against Clemson

obstacles for an opposing offense by taking chances and applying constant pressure.

Pressure is the name of the Carolina game, both offensively and defensively. Smith likes to send his athletes into a game with the purpose of attacking; he wants to take the action to the other team, rather than allow the foe to dictate the ebb and flow of the contest. Smith seeks to set the pace. His Tar Heels seek to make something happen. Thanks to Smith's philosophy of how basketball should be played, they have made plenty happen over the years.

ISSUES AND ANSWERS

Dean Smith has never been one to sit back and watch. He has left his mark on the game of basketball in many ways. Yet there are some areas in which the North Carolina coach feels that a new approach is needed.

For years, Smith has been a tireless proponent of making college freshmen ineligible for varsity competition in football and basketball. His position is that the practice, the travel, and the number of games played by varsity athletic teams place a huge burden of time and pressure on freshmen.

"The education, well-being, development, and maturation of the young student-athlete would be well served by the elimination of freshman eligibility in football and basketball in Division I," Smith said. "The principal reason I take this position is the need to make a strong statement to incoming freshmen that their academic work comes first in time and importance. The young student-athlete, like all students, must make the adjustment to living away from home, to a more demanding and competitive academic environment, and to a changed social setting. In addition to these adjustments, we have been asking the freshman athlete to give many hours of time and attention prematurely to another major dimension of his college life, the high-profile teams of football and basketball. It is common sense that the diversion of the student-athlete from what should be his primary focus in his freshman year is not in his best interests.

"Many do not realize the major difference in time required of the varsity athlete and the freshman before freshman eligibility was established by the NCAA in 1972. The varsity and freshmen practice about two hours a day in season. This practice is supposed to provide a healthy physical workout, improve skills, and foster enjoyable relationships among teammates. In addition to this practice time, however, a freshman playing on the varsity spends many hours with film review, frequent team meetings, travel for games, and media attention. If freshmen were ineligible for varsity competition, they would have the extra time for academics."

Smith listed several other benefits of freshman ineligibility. "It would validate a university's admission and academic-performance standards," he said, "since a student would not be eligible to compete in varsity athletics until he had completed a full year of academic work satisfactorily. Recruiting intensity should be reduced, because a player couldn't come in and supposedly turn a program around right away. The competitive balance we now enjoy in college basketball came about because of the C-average standard for admission, rather than freshman eligibility. The C-average standard became an NCAA rule about the same time that freshmen became eligible.

"There is no evidence that freshman ineligibility impairs the careers of future pro players," Smith said. "On the contrary, a pressure-free freshman year enhances the learning of the fundamentals in a sport and should improve chances for a good career.

Smith with John Kuester

"Those against freshman ineligibility have said it will cost more. In fact, economics played the major role in making freshmen eligible in 1972. However, we should be able to make this change for the good of the student-athlete without major added costs. In both football and basketball, a junior-varsity or freshman program would provide competition on a limited basis—five football games and 16 basketball games, as before 1973. Freshman programs would involve some variety of relatively minor costs, such as game officials. However, total equipment costs and the number of coaching positions allowed would not need to be increased. If some athletic directors were shown a way to save money by cutting out freshman eligibility, they would immediately approve, never once thinking about what's best for the young people involved.

"Practically all Division I institutions have an athlete in football or basketball as the least qualified student in any freshman class," Smith said. "For years, these schools have admitted student-athletes unprepared academically simply to help their teams win. It is shameful when a marginal student is admitted, is eligible to play each year, and then fails to graduate. We have alarming statistics involving excellent universities across the country in which many football and basketball players never graduate.

"I don't believe any nationally ranked basketball team has been helped more by freshman eligibility than we have at North Carolina. Yet even though over 95 percent of our lettermen do graduate, there is no question in my mind they would have been better served educationally to have been ineligible for varsity play as freshmen.

"Almost all of the problems of intercollegiate athletics— excessive commercialism, compulsion to win, and the whole success-failure thing—impinge directly upon the talented freshman student-athlete. If we are serious about wanting to minimize these adverse factors and place our primary concern on the student-athlete, we should eliminate freshman eligibility."

There has been great controversy in recent years over whether college athletes should receive monetary supplements to their scholarships in the form of spending money. Some who consider themselves purists of amateurism say that any kind of payment makes college athletes professionals, while others argue that a full scholarship takes care of a college education just as it was intended to, and that extra money is therefore not necessary.

Smith does not agree with either argument. "I'm still old-fashioned in that I'm not for college athletes being paid salaries," he said. "But we're already paying them by giving them scholarships. When you give a tuition grant, you are paying them. Now, I'm saying to give them the full grant-in-aid—tuition, fees, books, room, and board—and then something so they can go home or go out and buy a hamburger. Years ago, there was $15 a month laundry money—which was cut out quite awhile back—but that certainly wouldn't buy many hamburgers today. Let's say a player is here in Chapel Hill with absolutely no means of support from home—no money. He can't work—by NCAA rule—for nine months. Where is he going to get the money to buy a soft drink or a pizza? Other students can take a part-time job. I don't want athletes to be able to save money and put it in the bank. I would like to see them with a chance to be a regular student, though.

"It would be the fair thing to do to say $150 or $200 a month is part of their scholarship. The NCAA should take some of its tournament money and make it so poor kids—no matter what school they attend—could get the same amount of money. Every young person in college likes to go out once in a while. I think we've already said we believe in paying athletes, because we're giving them scholarships. If we're going to do that, it should be so that a youngster can be treated like any other student, based on need. Academic scholarships include some money in addition to education costs. There is more to a college education than class and study.

"The maximum payment would be $200 a month, based on need, with a minimum of $100," Smith suggested. "Athletes would provide their families' tax returns, and we could tell who's in the most need. The NCAA takes considerable amounts of revenue generated from basketball, then uses it for travel, committee meetings, nonrevenue sports—which I agree are worthwhile—but notice how well those administrators live when they take those trips for meetings. The meetings are always in some fairly exotic places. And then there's the student-athlete, who doesn't have the spare change for a hamburger, trying to scrape living expenses together."

Dean Smith

College athletics have grown in popularity to the point that they are almost a mania. Alumni, booster-club members, and fans of many universities are consumed with their teams' success. Smith feels such involvement is both dangerous and wrong.

"We're a victim of our society," he said. "Athletics is a front porch, but is not the most important part of college by any means. But sports sure are visible and affect a lot of things. In some places, the football coach has more power than the university president, and that's a sad commentary on both college athletics and society. There are demands of winning at all costs, and the eventual victim is the student-athlete, who sometimes finds what was promised as a tremendous opportunity turns out to be an avenue to exploitation.

"Academic abuse takes its worst form in the exploitation of young people, specifically in Division I football and basketball, the sports in which most alumni and fans insist upon their teams being number one. They want their school to win and often don't care how, even if it means cheating. At our university, they do care about honesty, but at so many places, if a team goes on probation, they ask, 'Who turned us in?' instead of trying to get at the heart of why the school was turned in to begin with. It is exploitive of young men to be admitted to an academic institution and work so hard to help their teams and schools prosper, and then to fail to receive the deserved assistance needed to graduate. Doctoring transcripts, giving credit for courses not taken, manipulating class ranks are of no benefit either to a young man interested in college athletics or to the integrity of an institution. The theory of many administrators and coaches is that a young man is better off for having been at college four years, whether or not he gets a degree. That may be true, but if that is to be the case, then the university would be doing a greater service by admitting someone who is not going to be a contributor in athletics—not a great running back or seven-foot basketball player."

One of the worst perils in college sports is the way some boosters and alumni offer money and other gifts to athletes, whether recruits or those already enrolled. "It's amazing how some universities bow down to their alumni," Smith said. "The value given to sports is too high. Americans seem to be obsessed with sports. I guess it's the success syndrome we're all tied to. People depend on sports when they don't have that inner affirmation of security or success. When we won the national championship in '82, we were flooded with letters saying God willed that kid [Fred Brown of Georgetown] to throw the ball to James [Worthy]. That's the same mentality, the same audacity, that God was on our side during World War II.

"We have a lot of things out of perspective," Smith continued. "Athletes and coaches are put on a pedestal, and what kind of respect do teachers get? There is no profession more important than the teaching profession. But they aren't paid accordingly."

From time to time, overzealous supporters of college athletic programs have even brought NCAA sanctions down on their universities. "Overenthusiastic boosters can be a big problem; they are at many schools. Fortunately, we haven't had that problem at the University of North Carolina. I think our alumni are proud that we are doing it right. The nice thing about Carolina is that they don't tell us what to do. They give scholarships, but they don't think that gives them the right to tell me when to go to four corners. They let us [coaches] run the programs. Nobody is powerful outside that could bother us."

Perhaps Smith's program is not susceptible to outside influences because it is so organized and disciplined, with players always knowing what is expected of them. "Discipline is a part of it," the UNC coach said. "We can all think back to the best teacher we ever had. Usually, it will be someone who was demanding. We are demanding at Carolina, and I think the players respect that later. We're all after the same goals.

Smith with Roy Williams

Photo by Hugh Morton

We make that clear when we're recruiting: 'You [the player] say you want to go to class, to get your degree. We're going to help you do those things.' Leadership is important. I know I'm responsible for all of our alumni. We make that very clear. That's why we don't let people know who we're recruiting. I think I'd have to know if one of our players were getting paid. First, I want car registrations. If they're on scholarship, they ought to be able to fill out a car-registration form. I know whether my players have a car or a stereo. I also know, for the most part, their family background. So I think I'd have a hard time not knowing if they were receiving money or anything else."

Smith feels college athletics have an obligation to set a good example. And that includes not prostituting big-time sports by participating in the sponsorship of products that are detrimental to youth. "I think we can control television more than we do," Smith said. "They know they have a good thing going in college basketball. We ought to be able to tell beer sponsors no, that they can't advertise during intercollegiate athletic contests. We have 10- and 11-year-olds watching ACC basketball games on Saturday afternoons. Beer ads make it seem like their product is just like a soft drink to these young kids coming up. And these kids end up with tragedies with alcohol and driving. Dick Schultz, the NCAA executive director now, agrees. We need to say, 'We might not make as much money, but we don't do beer ads.'"

Smith thinks the fact that the NCAA hasn't always adhered to high standards is a symptom of a larger problem. "I'm a little worried about our culture," he said. "In some ways, the sixties were nice, in that people were worried more about one another then. They seemed to feel that making a lot of money wasn't necessarily the answer to life. I certainly don't think it is. There is a lot of money in pro sports these days, and a large number of youngsters grow up hoping to play basketball in the NBA. We've been fortunate to have several of our Carolina players go on to the NBA, but we don't judge our work as coaches by how many we have in the pros. The chance of being an NBA player—out of all those playing high school basketball—is about 30,000 to one. It's an unrealistic goal. Basically, education is the way to advance. Certainly, education is our number-one priority at the University of North Carolina. The main thing in life is to enjoy what you're doing. I would tell young people that they can do this through education and in caring about others. They'll feel better about themselves and more gratified in life."

Dean Smith's stature as a college basketball coach has given him a forum for making his views on college athletics and other subjects heard and publicized. However, Smith feels that the important things he has to say—particularly about the cause of the student-athlete, which he has championed so strongly—have fallen on deaf ears for the most part. "I've grown tired after all these years," he said. "I have served on committees and have talked and talked about things we should do in college athletics to help our student-athletes. Some progress has been made, but it has been very little. I'm kind of burned out by it all."

MORE THAN A COACH—WHAT THE PLAYERS SAY

Organized sports have a handy device for judging the achievements of coaches. It is called a won-lost record. But such records only accurately measure surface success—how well a coach's team fares on the field or in the gym. However, if it is true that winning is not everything, that athletics within an educational environment are merely part of a network designed to prepare participants for their best possible futures, then much more is involved. That being the case, no one should be better able to assess coaches' success than their players.

Dean Smith's players are unequivocally bounteous in their praise for the North Carolina coach. Whether the players were full-blown stars or unknown substitutes, their feelings for Smith are positive.

A number of former Tar Heel basketball players expressed their feelings for their coach.

Billy Cunningham

Billy Cunningham played his entire varsity career at North Carolina under Smith. He was named the ACC player of the year as a senior, then went on to become a member of the NBA all-rookie team in 1966. He was a first-team all-NBA selection three straight years and was the ABA player of the year in 1973. He was an all-star in the NBA and ABA a total of six times. Cunningham coached the Philadelphia 76ers from 1978 to 1985, guiding that club to the NBA championship in 1983 while compiling a career winning percentage of .698.

Almost everyone closely connected with Smith talks about the Carolina coach's interest in his players. Cunningham was no exception, but he added a different perspective. "There's something about Coach Smith," Cunningham said. "He shows a great deal of loyalty, but I would say the thing about that loyalty which impressed me most while I was playing was the concern he had, not so much for his top player or number-two player, but for the last guy on the team, the last guy in terms of playing ability. Coach was as concerned about that guy as any other player, which proved his feelings were not in direct proportion to what a player did for the basketball team. A good example was Peppy Callahan, a friend of mine [and a two-year varsity player] whom Coach Smith helped while he was getting his master's degree. Coach was concerned about what a player was going to do with his life; he was concerned that we were going to class and doing well. And there have been so many cases after players did finish at Carolina that Coach Smith has helped those players get jobs, tried to help them get a step ahead in life. I don't know of many college coaches who have loyalty from their ex-players, and I don't know of any who have it to the degree Coach Smith does. The reason is the loyalty he shows the players."

Cunningham spoke about Smith's preference for character over talent. "The one major thing about him which influenced me," Cunningham said, "is the type of people he likes around

Billy Cunningham

him as players. He is a great believer in character, and I think he helps build character in young people. I remember some players who had problems, but Coach Smith always stood by them. He helped them develop their character. That carries over to the type of player he likes to recruit. I feel Coach Smith is more concerned with the player's character than anything else. He feels if the young man is a good person and a hard worker, then he can make up for maybe being a little less talented than another person. Coach won't even bother with an athlete if he has been a problem in high school, but that's not to say he won't help his players who have problems. He simply goes after a certain kind of person. This has influenced me as much as anything—in the type of people I like to surround myself with.

"But Coach has been an influence in another way, too. I remember basketball was almost secondary in the way he looked upon his players. He demanded that we go to school and get a degree. He knew basketball was a great thing, but it can come to a screeching halt sometimes; then it's finished. And how well I know that. [A serious knee injury and subsequent surgery shortened Cunningham's pro career.] Coach Smith tries to let his players know there is more to life than basketball.

"He has worked so hard at his craft, and he is really thought well of—in the college game and in the pros. Pro teams will take a chance on a Carolina player even if he might be a borderline prospect because of Coach Smith's reputation for turning out solid players. His players will do anything for him because of the way he is. I know I would do anything for him because of all he has done for me."

Jimmy Smithwick

Jimmy Smithwick graduated from North Carolina in 1966. During his career as a Tar Heel basketball player, he served mostly in a reserve capacity. He went on to attend medical

Jimmy Smithwick

school in Chapel Hill and is now a pediatrician in Laurinburg, North Carolina.

"I did not have a scholarship when I arrived at Carolina," Smithwick said. "I went out and played freshman ball, and Coach Smith gave me a scholarship, telling me I had earned it. I was never a starter on a full-time basis, but I never got the feeling that Jimmy Smithwick was a sub, therefore lower class on the team. Coach treated us as equals. It takes a special talent to be able to mold a group of high school stars into a team, and he has that talent. He made me feel I was always contributing. I started a few games my senior year when I really knew I wasn't starter material, but I got the chance because I had paid my dues. I remember starting one game at Raleigh, and that meant a lot to me. I had watched the Dixie Classic there when I was growing up, and that made Raleigh kind of special.

"One of the things I remember quite vividly was getting called in for a talk with Coach Smith. We had experienced a few bad games, and he called us in individually. Well, I thought he was really going to have this big talk with me about basketball and what I had to improve on. I sat down, and Coach handed me a book titled *Dear and Glorious Physician*. It was about the life of Luke. Now, this was right in the middle of basketball season, and here we were on a losing streak. But Coach Smith knew I was a premed student and that I was interested in medicine. He threw this book out and said, 'Listen, I want you to read this. I think you'll find it very interesting.' And this was what we talked about. At the time, I didn't realize the significance of that conversation; I was even sort of hacked off that we didn't talk about basketball. But that taught me a lot about Coach Smith."

Smithwick played for Carolina during what could be termed a rebuilding period. "Duke was the powerhouse then," Smithwick said, "but we all had confidence in what Coach Smith told us. Those weren't real strong teams; but since I have graduated, I've never had the feeling that just because I wasn't on one of the better Carolina teams, I was any less to Coach Smith. I heard him use the word *family* sometimes in talking about the program. He has so much loyalty and it stands out. I've talked to guys who played for other coaches, and many of them say their former coach wouldn't give them the time of day after they finished playing. I know of so many instances where Coach Smith has gone out of his way for me.

"Winning takes care of a lot of problems, but back when I was at Carolina, we weren't winning the way we should have been. A few of the players were talking about Coach behind his back, and I think he knew it was going on. Still, I know he went out of his way to help them get good jobs when they graduated. He knew those guys had not supported him, and yet he opened a lot of doors for them. It doesn't matter who you are; if you are one of Coach Smith's players, he calls you in as a senior and says, 'Let's sit down and talk about your future. How can I help you?'"

Recalling how orderly Smith's practices were, Smithwick said, "He had every minute planned—so many minutes for this and so many for that. He was scientific in his coaching. The most basic thing he stressed was defense, and I remember we'd work time after time on drills in which we'd try to keep a man from getting the ball inbounds. Then there was this one drill which was a killer. We had to squat, getting our butts down to the floor, and Coach would have us get up and down the floor that way. In six weeks, our muscles were like cinder blocks. The thing Coach Smith did was get down to defensive fundamentals, which so many of us didn't learn in high school.

"He really had his teams practice situations which might not be expected to come up normally. Then, sure enough, they would arise in a game, and we'd be prepared. We didn't always execute perfectly what we had practiced, but at least we were prepared. There's no doubt in my mind Coach Smith is worth 10 to 15 points on the bench. I can still clearly remember Coach anticipating things that were going to happen. Picture this: you're in a tight spot, and here's this guy bending down with his team, smiling, just as calm as can be. That was Coach Smith, and he impressed me so much that way. Whether we were up two or down five, he was the same. He wasn't the type to show anger at players either. He didn't jerk you out the minute you did something stupid. Later on, when we'd be watching the films of that game, he would say something positive, like, 'Here's what you should have done,' but he never got on the players.

"I often wondered if Coach took many psychology courses," Smithwick said. "He could sure teach it, I know that. I've been out of school 24 years, and he still seems interested in me. There's no way there is a finer man, not to my way of thinking. Playing for Coach Smith meant more to me than anything else I've done."

Rusty Clark

Franklin "Rusty" Clark has often been credited by Smith for being a vital factor in North Carolina's basketball resurgence. Smith's first legitimate big man, he performed extremely well in a number of crucial games. He could have played professional basketball, but he chose to attend medical school instead. He is now a thoracic surgeon in his hometown of Fayetteville, North Carolina.

With Clark headed for med school, his schedule was much more rigorous than that of the average student. He remembers how his coach made his academic life much less complicated than it might have been. "I was academically oriented," Clark recalled. "I was interested in studying and enjoyed my educational opportunities. One thing Coach Smith told me which proved absolutely true was that he considered my education foremost and basketball second. Now, every player in the country hears that, but not many coaches mean it. While I was at Chapel Hill, many a practice was rearranged or re-

Rusty Clark

scheduled because I got out of chemistry lab at a different time, or I had a physics lab which met at a certain time, or my organic lecture was postponed. This was done for other players, too, but I had a lot of afternoon labs. Coach Smith would adjust practice often depending on my labs. He never asked me to skip a lab. In fact, if I was at practice at a time I normally would have been at class or lab, Coach Smith wanted to know what had happened and might ask, 'Hey, are you cutting something?' I appreciated his attitude. He never made it hard for me to get my education; he made it easy. He means what he says about his players getting an education; it's not just public relations stuff. I know because I personally experienced that type of situation.

"Coach is known for his honesty," Clark said, "but he believes in mutual trust, too. For example, he never questioned any of us players. If one said he had an injured ankle, he was excused from practice. He was good in many ways. I remember a couple of times I was really down on basketball, or there were times I wasn't doing what I should have been doing. Coach Smith would talk with me and would help me straighten things out. Like, he would say, 'In life, you've got to do certain things to be successful. If you want to be successful, you need to reevaluate what you're doing—if you don't, it's your business. But if you want to, there are certain things society expects of you and maybe that I expect of you as a member of this team. You really need to do these things if you're going to be a productive and successful player.'

"Coach Smith is an interesting person," Clark said. "I used to talk with him about the philosophy of religion. Those were some of the most interesting discussions I had with him. . . . He carries many of his philosophies over into practice. That appealed to me. He was a unique man to me. He allowed me freedoms and gave me room to grow, making me totally free to do many things and have a rich college career."

There are those who feel the coach's role in athletic success is overemphasized, but Clark feels the opposite may be true.

"When a team wins consistently, luck can be discounted. Perhaps the team is making its own luck, but a degree of skill is involved in being able to do that. The team wins most of the close ones. Is it the players? I don't think that can be the key; I think it is the skill of the coach. Coach Smith's skill is proven by his record. He wins every year, and he wins the close ones. He loses some, too, but the percentages are overwhelming in his favor. While I was at Carolina, we won the ACC regular season, the ACC Tournament, and the Eastern Regional three straight years. I know there were other teams in the eastern part of the nation which were as good, if not better, than us. Maybe we made our own luck, though, and see, it's not luck anymore. A person tosses a coin, and 50 percent of the time it's going to be heads; but when it's heads 90 percent of the time, you better look and make sure there aren't heads on both sides of the coin. When that happens, somebody is making the difference. With that kind of percentage, it's in the toss and not luck. Take any college nowadays, and look at the first 10 players. There probably will not be that much difference between the teams in terms of raw talent. It comes down to a coaching game. The guy who wins most of the games is not winning really with the superstar, because every team has its superstar. He is winning with the other guys. That's where Coach Smith gets his mileage—he has superstars, but he knows how to use his other guys.

"He has always given responsibility to the second team. He does this better than anyone I've seen, and he gets a lot out of his reserves by putting them in a game at crucial times. That's a tremendous confidence booster. When a coach puts a guy in with 30 seconds left and the team ahead by 25 points, he might as well put in the water boy. That doesn't do anyone any good. And if a coach thinks he's doing a player a favor by using him like that, he's not. Coach Smith would take guys who had run second team all week in practice; there would be six minutes left in a game, with us down by two points, and he'd put a member of the second team in. More often than not, Coach would get an outstanding performance from that guy.

"The most impressive thing to me about Coach Smith is his respect for the individual. He never yelled and screamed at players or said, 'Hey, you dirty bum, c'mon, let's hustle,' or 'You're not putting out,' and stuff like that. I never saw Coach pull anyone for messing up, unless it was a violent action like starting a fight, or if a player got a technical. A player never came out for taking a bad shot or making a bad pass. In fact, it was usually quite the opposite—Coach would be quick to put a player back in or keep him in when he was having a rough time. That was a confidence builder.

"Coach Smith ran a tight ship in practice," Clark remembered. "He became angry sometimes, but even in a moment of anger, he always maintained his cool. . . . That is incredible in athletics. He is an amazing man."

Bob McAdoo

Bob McAdoo was at Carolina only one season, but he was an immediate star. He was an all-American selection, and he helped the Tar Heels reach the Final Four of the NCAA Tournament. He went on to be named the NBA rookie of the year in 1973 and the league's most valuable player in 1975. He led the NBA in scoring three straight years, helped the Los Angeles Lakers win a championship in 1985, and concluded his NBA career with the Philadelphia 76ers the next year.

When McAdoo had the opportunity to turn pro rather than play his senior year with the Tar Heels, Smith did not try to hold back his instant sensation. That made a lasting impression on McAdoo.

"I remember Coach Smith telling me that if they offered this certain amount of money, he'd have had to take it himself if he were a player," McAdoo said. "But he told me to get what I was worth, not to take anything less. He felt a college degree was good, but he told me a college degree wouldn't guarantee

Bob McAdoo

the kind of money the pros were paying at this time. He gave me things to think about and was very supportive; he was behind me all the way. He was never negative and didn't try to talk me out of going pro. Coach told me to do what I thought right for me and my family. I'm sure a lot of coaches might have tried to talk me out of turning pro, and the fact that Coach Smith didn't do that really impressed me. I saw right then that he wasn't selfish like a lot of the coaches I've seen since then. He was strictly there for the players' benefit, and he wanted what was best for my welfare and future."

McAdoo not only departed Carolina under unusual circumstances, he arrived the same way—as the only transfer Smith has ever accepted. McAdoo recalls being welcomed without hesitation. "I felt right at home from the start," he said. "It was an honor to be the first transfer Coach Smith had taken. I was treated like everybody else, and I liked that. I fit in, and the players were all real nice to me, but Coach Smith was a big reason for things going so smoothly. He is a smart man, and he knew how the other players might feel, so he had everything and everyone prepared.

"I learned a lot of basketball at Carolina even though I was there just one year. Coach Smith taught me the fundamentals of the game better than I had ever had them taught. I had gotten away from fundamentals and was playing on natural ability alone. I needed to get back to basics. When I got to Carolina, we worked on the finer points of basketball—boxing out on defense, overplaying your man on defense, and going back door for layups. My defense really improved. In fact, I used my background playing for Coach Smith to shut up my critics in the NBA. Because I was such a successful offensive player in the pros, a high scorer, some people said I couldn't play defense. I told them, 'Hey, Dean Smith doesn't have players who can't play defense.'

"Coach Smith was a fine teacher, and he is a fine man—the finest. I still talk with him when tough times come up, and he gives me the same kind of pep talk as when I was at Carolina.

He tells me to keep my chin up and do the best I can—those are the type things that are good to hear. Coach Smith can always pick me up. He always sent cards, congratulating me on good games I had in the NBA, and he came to my father's funeral. I remember those things. I am one of his family just as if I had been at Carolina four years. Dean Smith is my friend—a good friend."

Mitch Kupchak

Mitch Kupchak was one of the most determined athletes ever to play for Smith. A talented big man who always hustled despite back problems, Kupchak was only the second Tar Heel to grab 1,000 career rebounds, and he left Carolina among the school's top-10 all-time scorers. He was an all-American selection and was the ACC player of the year as a senior. In the NBA, he exhibited the same energetic style that had made him a collegiate standout. Kupchak began his pro career with the Washington Bullets, then played with the Los Angeles Lakers before his career was ended by injuries. He is currently the Lakers' assistant general manager.

"Dean Smith has been one of the most influential persons in my life," Kupchak said. "My father is the most influential male in my life by far, but Coach and my high school coach are next. Coach Smith is much more than a coach. I remember when he called to find out how my back was doing [when Kupchak was in the NBA in the late seventies]. I had had surgery on it, and his calling really made me feel good. Heck, if I was an insurance salesman, I felt I could have gone out and sold $100,000 worth. I felt like I was dynamite after talking to him. It's not so much talking to Coach, I guess, because one can't talk to just anybody and feel that way. It's what led up to that certain time. It was the past several years and the way he treated me—the mutual respect we have built.

"I remember my first or second year at Carolina," Kupchak said. "I had some problems, and I went to Coach Smith. He

Mitch Kupchak

was like a father figure. I already had a lot of respect for him as a coach, but when he treated me the way he did, this certain feeling built. I began to feel very close to him. It seemed I had more problems than most other players when I was in college. My back caused most of them. Coach Smith was extraspecial to me—he took a very sincere interest in my health. And he wasn't really very concerned in my playing basketball, not as much as in my being healthy. Normally, when you're a player, you go in and talk to Coach Smith about playing basketball and about your schoolwork, and you don't have a whole lot more to say. But I had problems, like my back, and I spent a lot of time talking about things which didn't have anything to do with basketball.

"I can never knock another coach," Kupchak said, "but I can very easily speak about Coach Smith. I've talked to a lot of other players in the pros. I have talked to them about their college coaches, and many of them never hear from their former coaches—they haven't since they played their last college game. That's like the college used somebody for four years, then said, 'Now you're on your own.' I wouldn't like that."

Smith is known for teaching his players values that are more important off the basketball court than on it. Kupchak reflected on this. "So much of what he taught me sticks with me, and it started on a basketball court. Things that he insists on during practice and basketball-related things are valuable in later life. Things like being prompt, appreciating what someone else does for you, not abusing a person in something you might say—little things like that. Things like the way we thanked each other on the basketball court, or never being late for practice—they carry over into life. I remember Coach Smith told us if someone is late to meet you, then that person is telling you his time is more important than yours, and that's why that person was late. It should never be that way, Coach told us, because no one's time is any more important than anyone else's. No one was late for practice at Carolina when I was there. It would seem that might be forgotten quickly, but you don't forget it. Once you've played for Coach Smith, what he teaches stays with you. The promptness thing is an example."

Because of the difficulties with his back, Kupchak played with pain during much of his college career. There was one particularly memorable incident Kupchak will probably never forget. "I remember it was my junior year, and I was having a lot of problems with my back," he said. "We played at Clemson on a Saturday night and lost. Coach Smith had arranged for me to have this procedure done the next morning, Sunday morning. It was called an epidural block, and it was to be done at Memorial Hospital in Chapel Hill. Well, after playing at Clemson, it was around three in the morning when we arrived back in Chapel Hill. My meeting with the doctor was scheduled for eight-thirty. I got up and got over to the hospital in time. What was involved was an injection, a block, in my back. It was kind of like having an enzyme injected into my nervous system . . . and the enzyme was supposed to deaden or block the pain impulses and stop the pain. It was a type of surgery. And when we were getting ready to go into the operating room, Coach Smith showed up. There it was, eight-thirty in the morning, and Coach had had very little sleep, plus he had so many things to do—and he was there to be with me. He put on one of those gowns and one of those masks, and he came into the operating room. He stayed there and watched me through the whole thing, keeping his hand on my shoulder. That meant a lot to me. I mean, I expected to have the surgery done and remain in the hospital, and I would have just appreciated Coach visiting me. But I was a long way from home, and I didn't know anyone in the hospital; so it really meant a great deal for Coach to do what he did.

"He shows his interest in his players in so many ways. I was impressed immediately when he first visited me to recruit me, and I am much more impressed now. He is a great friend and a great man."

Walter Davis

Walter Davis was the NBA rookie of the year as a member of the Phoenix Suns in 1978. He has been selected an NBA all-star several times, and he has been a second-team all-NBA choice twice. One of the most underrated players ever at North Carolina, he was an all-ACC selection as a senior. He ranks as one of the most versatile Tar Heels ever, having finished his career among the top-10 all-time leaders in scoring, rebounds, and assists.

Davis played solid basketball throughout his four-year UNC career, but members of the press seemed to expect even more of him. There were some frustrating times for the graceful, quiet man who would come to be known as "the Greyhound" in his early NBA years. "Yes, there were times that it bothered me that no one seemed to notice or appreciate my contributions to the team," Davis said. "That was one way Coach Smith meant so much to me. I was being overlooked and was compared to David Thompson. Coach told me I didn't have to prove anything to other people, just to the coaching staff and to my teammates. He told me I had already done that and that he had confidence in me. That helped a great deal at that time in my career, but Coach Smith has helped me in so many different ways over the years. To me, he has always been a good example of somebody to look up to and try to be like. He has shown me a lot of kindness.

"In basketball, the things Coach taught me were the main reasons I have made it in the pros. The way he treated me as a person was important, too. I remember how honest he was when talking to me about going to Carolina. He simply told me if I did the job, I would play, and he said guys who could play defense would play a lot. He just laid things right on the line. I knew what I had to do from the start—even before I went to Carolina."

Davis reflected upon a couple of incidents from his days in

Walter Davis

Chapel Hill. "I wasn't too good at taking charges when I first went to Carolina," he remembered. "Well, one day in practice, I took a charge. Coach Smith came running up and shook my hand. He said, 'Walter, you drew a charge. You're not hurt, are you?' I told him I wasn't, and I felt great. It was kind of like jumping in water for the first time. There was this thing Coach would do after games we won. He would come around and actually thank all the players for playing hard, for giving it our best, and for making the win possible. That certainly wasn't necessary or expected, but I thought it was extra thoughtful. Then there was the night he threw the rock group Fleetwood Mac out of Carmichael. That was kind of funny to me, but it showed how serious Coach is about his practices. Fleetwood Mac was going to perform in the gym, and one of the guys from the group was tuning a piano. Coach likes it quiet when he's saying something, so he told that guy he had to go. We always talked about how Coach Smith threw that group out.

"Coach Smith is still helping me. . . . He has always been there to talk with during some tough times. I want to try to help him if I can. With him, basketball at Carolina is a family thing. I really look up to Coach Smith a whole lot; in fact, I look up to him as much as I do my father."

John Kuester

John Kuester was the ultimate unsung hero at North Carolina. He finally received recognition for his contributions during his senior year. En route to helping the Tar Heels reach the NCAA championship game, Kuester was named most valuable player in both the ACC Tournament and the East Regional. He had a short NBA career, then turned to college coaching, heading programs at Boston University and George Washington.

"Dean Smith is the reason I went to North Carolina," Kuester said. "He had such a wide variety of knowledge, and

John Kuester

when he talked to me, he could talk about a wide range of things and not just basketball. When I was recruited, some coaches told me flat-out that I would start for them. Coach Smith didn't do that. He was just very honest, telling me there was a great opportunity for me at Carolina. I thought that over, and to hear a man of his stature say what he did made me really respect him. From that point on, I definitely was going to Carolina.

"It was a big adjustment for me when I went to college, but Coach Smith made things easier. He helps monitor freshmen and guides them into positive situations. The big thing, though, was that his door was always open for his players. Also, he had a lot of discipline, especially on the basketball court. As freshmen, we had to chase balls which would bounce away during practice. That might sound like a dumb thing to some people, but it adds discipline, particularly for those not used to doing something like that. It also helped make everyone equal, since every player on the team had done the same thing at one time or another. Coach never had to raise his voice to get his point across, and he never cursed; he had our undivided attention.

"I looked back after having been at Carolina a couple of years, and I realized I never could have been as happy anywhere else. The people on the coaching staff are wholesome people, and that impressed me because I'm from a family which is down-to-earth. I've always worked hard, and I had always gone after loose balls on the court and clapped for my teammates. That was before I even knew Carolina did those things. I imagined myself doing those things for other big colleges, and there wasn't another one which I could honestly say would have appreciated my talents as much as Carolina. Coach Smith always appreciated effort and hustle."

Kuester remembers being told by former Tar Heel George Karl that a player's relationship with Smith and the Carolina program would make him want to return to Chapel Hill. "I loved my home in Richmond, Virginia," Kuester said, "but sure enough, it's always great getting back to see Coach Smith. When I was a rookie in the NBA, he would call and make sure I was doing okay. He doesn't put up a front; he is genuine. He is interested in his players. I don't care if a player sits on the bench at Carolina for four years, Coach Smith will be good to that player. He even helps team managers just as if they were all-Americans. I roomed with a manager, and I know Coach helped him. I can't believe Coach Smith has the time to do all he does, but I think he really likes to help his former players. He even went over my pro contracts with me. He does the little things, and the little things are what make a person in life. People who don't know Coach Smith can't believe all they hear about him. Some think he is a fake, and some resent it because they've heard so many good things. The shame of it is that all the players I know can't say the same things about their college coaches as I can. Many of those players only have a former coach; I have a lifelong friend."

In remembering the intensive preparation he and his Tar Heel teammates underwent, Kuester said, "Coach had us ready for all types of game situations. If this player fouled out or couldn't play, this other player knew he was to take a certain spot. There were no surprises. That was great coaching as far as I was concerned. Coach Smith doesn't just shine on his starters; he concentrates on the whole team. When we walked into a game, we believed we could win if we did what Coach wanted us to do."

Carolina lost to Marquette in the 1977 NCAA championship contest, the final game in Kuester's college career. The dressing-room scene following the disappointing defeat was one he will not forget. "I was a senior, and that made the loss especially tough because I didn't have another chance," Kuester said. "I was doing okay, though; I hadn't broken up or anything. I had made up my mind not to get upset. I was fine, not real emotional, and then Coach Smith came up. Remember, he had never won the title, but there he was smiling and keeping himself together. He went up to all our seniors and said, 'Thanks for the four years you gave me.' That got to me. And then I bumped into him in the bathroom, and it was all over. I boohooed, and it was like I was crying on my dad's shoulder. Coach Smith hugged me, and the whole thing was one of the most touching things to ever happen to me. I was so discouraged because we lost when we had wanted to win the championship for Coach Smith, and there he was consoling us and thanking us. He is an amazing and unique person."

Phil Ford

Phil Ford was the NBA rookie of the year in 1979, having played a major role in the Kansas City Kings' transformation from a last-place team into a playoff participant. While at North Carolina, he was a three-time all-American, and he was named the college player of the year as a senior. He was also honored as ACC player of the year and ACC athlete of the year. Ford owns the Tar Heel career scoring record and is second to Kenny Smith in assists. After several years in the pros and a few in business, he returned to Chapel Hill as an assistant to his former coach.

As a high-scoring prep standout in Rocky Mount, North Carolina, Ford attracted college recruiters in droves. He clearly remembers Smith's first visit. "When I met him, I had already known he was a great coach," Ford said, "but after getting to talk with him, I knew he was a great man, too. He didn't promise me anything, and I knew that if he didn't, then he wouldn't with anybody else. He became a father figure to me. He had a real good one-on-one relationship with all of our players. He cared about our development as citizens. I think there are a lot of good coaches in the United States, but what separates Coach Smith from the others is the way he cares

Phil Ford

about his players. He isn't a season coach. Some coaches are a player's friend only from October to March, but not him.

"I can't pick one thing which I think makes Coach Smith such a great coach. It's a combination. He is a tremendous teacher, as shown by the number of players he has go on to the pros. Every time I went to practice in my four years at Carolina, I think I walked off the court a little better basketball player. Practices were not long, but they were hard. We worked. I don't think there was anything we didn't go over in practice. I was surprised on the college level that we'd get as involved in fundamentals as we did. Some of those little things I thought were so easy to do weren't really that easy. We practiced those things, and I think that gave us an edge. Defensive techniques, of course, were big with Coach; the longer a player stays at Carolina, the better defensive player he becomes. The special kind of way Coach has with his players is fantastic—that helps make him great, too. He respects his players, which is one reason they respect him so much. He is always under control, and that means a lot. He never gets rattled; when he stays calm and cool, that rubs off. Everybody else in the gym can be screaming in a tight situation, but there is Coach in control, always running the show. That makes the players feel more relaxed. And Coach Smith never gets upset with a player unless it's for not hustling. That's because he feels it's disrespectful to the other players. But he'll never say anything about a physical mistake."

Ford recalled one game sequence that demonstrated Smith's patience and his basketball intuition. "I laugh when I think about it," Ford said. "We were playing up at Virginia my senior year, and Coach told me to run a certain play. Now, as the quarterback on the court, I had the option to run another play if I felt I should, and that's what I did. The one I called didn't work, then the one he called worked the next time we came down the floor. But Coach Smith didn't get upset; he never blames a player. That type of attitude and support makes every player want to give him everything."

Mike O'Koren

Mike O'Koren was an instant hit at Carolina, playing a large part in the Tar Heels' trek to the 1977 national championship game, his performance earning him a spot on the NCAA all-tournament team as a freshman. O'Koren was named to numerous all-American teams during his UNC career. He ranks among the school's all-time leaders in field-goal percentage, points, rebounds, and assists. He played several years in the NBA and is now with the New Jersey Nets in radio and public relations.

When O'Koren was being courted by college recruiters, Smith made a pitch unlike any the New Jersey high school star had heard. "I remember the way he talked to me," O'Koren said, "and the reason I liked Coach Smith so much was that he was interested in Mike O'Koren the person, not Mike O'Koren the basketball player. I made up my mind and committed to North Carolina early. Today, Coach Smith is still interested in me, and he was all through my four years at Carolina. When he first came to my family's house, Coach Smith told me that he was interested in my getting a diploma at the University of North Carolina, and he said the diploma came before athletics. A lot of coaches will say that, but Coach is sincere. The fact that he wants that diploma for all his players says something for him as a person."

When O'Koren was a sophomore, some distasteful posters about his poor complexion surfaced in gyms around the ACC, and they upset the young Tar Heel immensely. "The fans at a couple of places on the road really came down on me," he recalled. "It didn't mix well with me because I didn't think basketball was that important for people to get on a person for the way he looks or something like that. I sort of get emotional at times, and this really hurt me. It hurt my feelings— knocked me for a loop. Well, I went in and talked to Coach Smith about it, and I came out a new man, in a way. It was just the way Coach came across—what he said to me. I really

Mike O'Koren

Jimmy Black

Photo by Hugh Morton

needed help at that time, and he really helped a lot; he cared. I appreciated that.

"There was another time I was especially grateful to Coach Smith for the way he is. My mother broke her back when I was a sophomore. My brother came to me after a game and told me what had happened. Coach asked me would I like to go home, and I said I would. I went back home and missed some practices. I made it back for our next game, but Coach wouldn't have been upset if I had missed that. He was so concerned. Now, obviously, any coach would be concerned if one of his players' mothers broke her back, but it was just the way Coach Smith treated me during this time. It was always clear to me that basketball isn't most important with Coach, and it was also clear that he doesn't expect it to be with the players either.

"My junior year, the media came down on me for scoring only 14.8 points a game, and there was a lot of stuff written about my having a bad season. It shouldn't have bothered me, but it did. I went to Coach Smith, and he straightened me out right away. He told me I had done everything he had wanted and that I didn't have to prove anything to anybody else. I look back, and those things which seemed big really weren't, although they seemed important at the time. Coach never acted as though a problem of mine wasn't important. He always had time for me."

Jimmy Black

Jimmy Black's career at North Carolina did not begin on a bright note, but it certainly ended gloriously. In his first couple of years, Black was criticized by the fans and the media for being an erratic passer and poor shooter. Smith never listened to such things, of course, and Black became the extension of his coach on the court. As a senior, Black was the quarterback and spark as the Tar Heels won the national title. He served as an assistant coach at St. Joseph's before becoming an assistant coach at the University of South Carolina.

"Coach never got down on me, even though lots of other people did," Black recalled. "Everything was always positive. That's the way it was with the whole team. If Coach Smith recruits somebody, it's because he feels that player can help the Carolina team. Every player gets a fair shot. It's then up to the individual to make the best of that opportunity. Coach never gave up on me."

Black remembers rigorous practices under Smith, who believes in work and 100-percent effort. "He could get after players, but he was always there to support us and correct us," said the former UNC point guard. "And he could get pretty upset. He has tossed guys out of practice. If players weren't putting out or if they were getting on one another, he'd send 'em out. Getting on a teammate or jawing with one another was the ultimate sin; he wouldn't put up with that. And he wouldn't put up with less than total effort. His approach was business as usual. It was the same in March and April as on October 15. Coach Smith didn't change or tighten up because games were bigger or because it was the NCAAs."

Now, as a coach himself, Black admires Smith more than ever. "He helps his players not just when they're playing, but when they get out. He'll consult, take time to give advice, and do whatever he can. He doesn't just say he'll do it; he lives it."

James Worthy

James Worthy was one of North Carolina's all-time great basketball players. He was a consensus all-American in 1982, his final season with the Tar Heels. That was his junior year, when he led UNC to the NCAA championship by scoring 28 points against Georgetown in the title game. He was named the Helms Foundation's national co-player of the year, sharing the honor with Virginia's Ralph Sampson. Worthy was also first-team all-ACC and the ACC Tournament's most valu-

James Worthy

Photo by Hugh Morton

able player in 1982. Following the 1981–82 season, he announced he would bypass his senior year to turn pro. He was picked first in the NBA draft and went on to make the league's all-rookie team as a member of the Los Angeles Lakers. An NBA all-star, he played a major role in the Lakers' championships in the 1980s.

When Worthy was a high school senior in Gastonia, North Carolina, most sports followers in the state expected him to become a Tar Heel, since he had grown up attending Dean Smith's summer basketball camps and seemed a natural for the UNC program. Worthy shopped around before making his decision. "Dean Smith was the difference," he said. "I liked Carolina anyway, but my family and I were so impressed with the way Coach treats his players and the way he does things."

Recalling his decision to forgo his senior season at UNC—a decision his coach helped him make—Worthy again spoke highly of Smith. "He really helped a lot in my decision. He sat me down and told me all the pros and cons of leaving Carolina. He told me it would be different from college, that there wouldn't be as much caring in the pros. He encouraged me to go if the situation was right, but he didn't put any pressure on me either way.

"But that's the way Coach Smith always has been," Worthy recalled. "He was always extremely honest with me and with all of his players. That's one of the reasons he has been as successful as he has. Guys at Carolina know they can trust him completely."

Looking back, Worthy said, "I have been fortunate to be a part of a great Laker organization, but I have missed the caring I got at Carolina. I knew Coach Smith was always going to do the right thing. My development as a person was as important to him as my development as a player."

It is still meaningful to Worthy that he helped win Smith a national title. "Winning the NCAA championship is great anyway," he said, "but helping get one for Coach was really important. He has always been a champion as a coach. He deserved a championship."

Worthy is one of a large number of former Tar Heels who return to Chapel Hill each summer to work at Smith's camp. "It's a lot of fun," he said. "I remember when I was a kid in the camp myself. It's great seeing lots of the guys again. And most of all, it's always great seeing Coach Smith. He has meant a lot to me and my family."

Matt Doherty

As a sophomore, Matt Doherty was a starter on North Carolina's 1982 NCAA championship team. He was a solid player from the time he became a Tar Heel. Although he hit some big baskets during his career, Doherty was most noted for doing the often-unappreciated things like setting screens, boxing out on rebounds, passing, and playing tough defense. After working on Wall Street for a few years, he returned to basketball in 1989 as an assistant coach at Davidson.

"Dean Smith has always been someone I respected a great deal and whom I immensely wanted to please," Doherty said. "I feel very fortunate to have been touched by him. He is an exceptional person that players naturally feel a tremendous loyalty toward. People who don't know Coach can't appreciate him because they don't know what he's all about. He is a rare combination, one of the brightest people you'd ever meet and one of the toughest competitors you could find. He isn't just smart, though; he is streetwise in terms of savvy about life and what's going on.

"At Carolina, and because of Coach Smith, playing basketball is not just a four-year deal; it's for a lifetime. I always thought a lot of the man, but what he did means even more to me now that I'm out of school. A player at North Carolina doesn't realize the impact playing for Dean Smith is going to have in later life. He has so much admiration and respect everywhere that he opens doors for his former players in

Matt Doherty

Photo by Hugh Morton

terms of jobs and opportunities. And the things you learn from him carry over into life—the integrity and organization.

"Being in the coaching profession myself now, I appreciate Coach Smith even more," Doherty said. "The way he does things, the way he motivates, the confidence he always has in his team, the positive approach—all of those things tie into the success he has had as a coach. And he has discipline. With Coach, you know that if you do something wrong, you'll be punished. But not many Carolina players step out of line. It wasn't that way on the court, though; Coach Smith never jumped all over anyone for making a bad pass or taking a bad shot."

Doherty recalled a game experience that left him a lasting impression of his coach. "We were down 16 to Virginia and had taken a time-out," he said. "We were sitting there, wondering what Coach Smith would say with us so far behind. He looked up at us with a twinkle in his eye, smiled, and said, 'Wouldn't it be nice to come back and win this one? Let's accept this challenge.' We did. We came back and won."

Something his former coach said helped convince Doherty to turn his attention from Wall Street to coaching. "Coach always said that if you're doing something you like, you'll be compensated," Doherty remembered, "whether in money or pleasure. Those words helped me make the decision to be where I am now, and I've never been happier. As a coach, I'd love to be just a fraction of what Dean Smith is. Then I'd feel I was a big success."

J. R. Reid

J. R. Reid was a two-time all-American in his three-year stay at Carolina and was a consensus selection as a sophomore. He was first-team all-ACC in 1988, and he was named the ACC Tournament's most valuable player in 1989 for his role in leading the Tar Heels to the championship. With Smith's help, he

J. R. Reid

Photo by Hugh Morton

turned pro after his junior year and received a lucrative contract from the Charlotte Hornets.

Reid has always been an emotional player and a very competitive one. During his college career, some fans and media members speculated that Reid was not happy at Carolina and that he and his coach did not always get along. "That's just not true," Reid said. "I wanted to play, and sometimes when I didn't, I was upset. My last year, when I was injured, Coach Smith set up a rotation, and when I came back, there weren't as many minutes for me as there had been before. I didn't like it, but he was the coach. I wasn't mad at him; it wasn't a personal thing. I've always thought he is a great coach, and that never changed.

"Dean Smith is the main reason I went to Carolina in the first place," Reid said. "My parents liked the fact that winning isn't everything with him and that he wants his athletes to also be students. His teaching has helped me a whole lot. Practices at Carolina are very tough; the NBA almost seems easy in comparison. I broke some rules when I was there, and I paid the penalty. I knew beforehand what the rules and punishment were. Coach Smith is strict; he expects his players to do certain things. But he's fair. And I'm already seeing how all the things he tried to teach me are helping. Like not being late. It's a part of growing up. When he punished me, though, he made it clear there were no hard feelings. And there have never been any on my part."

Reid recalls seeing Smith more than a little upset. "Yes, if we weren't doing what we were supposed to at practice—not concentrating or going as hard as we could—he didn't like it. He wouldn't put up with not putting out. I got thrown out of some practices. Sometimes, he told us all to leave.

"But he's definitely behind all his players. He went out of his way to help me when I was considering passing up my senior year to enter the NBA draft. Coach Smith checked out everything. He felt it was a good time for me to go pro because he said there was a lot of money to be made. He had it put in my contract [as he had previously done with Bob McAdoo, James Worthy, and Michael Jordan] that I would be paid a bonus if I got my degree within three years. And I will, because I was only a few courses short when I left. My parents weren't for me leaving after my junior year until Coach showed them how it was for the best. It would have been easy for him not to do that, and I would probably have stayed at Carolina. But he was doing what was best for me and my future. He was always concerned. His door was always open, and he was there for us players. I talked with him a lot. And I've talked with him several times since I left school. As time goes on, I realize how good our relationship is.

"When you're at Carolina, Coach is trying to make you a better player. You become closer to him, I think, when you leave. He is a real friend."

PRAISE FROM PEERS

Recognition by one's peers is the most meaningful applause a person can receive, no matter what the profession. Jealousy may infiltrate the ranks, but peer assessment is generally the most valid of all.

The coaching profession is certainly no different. Coaches are the only true experts in their sports. They are the ones who possess the expertise to analyze fellow coaches. They alone really know what it takes to win, to run a solid program, to teach athletes how to play, and to motivate them to perform well. Coaches know the work involved and the ingredients necessary to attain success.

And so it is a huge testimonial that Dean Smith is held in such high esteem by basketball coaches across the nation. Probably no other coach is in greater demand at clinics. Smith's advice is sought by collegiate and high school coaches, and his ability to teach the game is highly respected by the pros. Pat Riley, the former coach of the Los Angeles

Lakers, once said, "We always look for players from North Carolina. If we could draft players from North Carolina every year, we'd do it. You know they know how to play. The players are so full of character, like James Worthy and Michael Jordan. I think James's success [with the Lakers] is based directly on how he was coached in college. I have a lot of respect for Coach Smith. I'm the beneficiary of a man who has taught all these guys how to play the game. When they come to the pros, they're refined. They're ready to step right in." Former Chicago Bulls Coach Kevin Loughery credited Smith for the way Jordan has handled his immense fame: "Michael has had the most media hype I've seen in pro basketball, and I was around Dr. J for three years. Michael has handled it extremely well. It is a tremendous tribute to the way Dean Smith, who is one of the greatest coaches of all time, handled this guy. You can see his training."

When Dean Smith speaks about basketball, other coaches listen. Smith is well respected for his innovations, his organization, his team concept, and his ethical standards. He has been called the modern-day coach who has made the greatest impact upon his game. It in no way downplays the monumental records of John Wooden and Adolph Rupp to say that Smith has become the most copied coach in the game.

Numerous coaches have spent lengthy sessions with Smith discussing approaches to basketball and the way to build a strong, exciting, and reputable program. Coaches often visit or phone to ask Smith's opinions on various phases of the game, and as time allows, the Tar Heel coach unselfishly obliges. Because of his willingness to share his ideas, Smith is both popular and highly regarded.

A number of coaches from the collegiate ranks offered their insights.

John Thompson

John Thompson has enjoyed great success as the Georgetown University coach, directing his team to an NCAA championship while making the Hoyas a perennial national power.
His program is among the most outstanding in college basketball. Thompson has known Dean Smith for many years. He
served as one of Smith's assistant coaches on the 1976 United
States Olympic team, then went on to become the head coach
of the United States team in the 1988 Olympics.

"When I joined [Dean Smith] for the Olympics," Thompson
recalled, "I had already known him for a long time and had
come to respect him a great deal. I felt working with Dean in
the Olympics was a very great experience for me, one of the
highlights of my career. Even in the way he asked me to be his
assistant, Dean showed what kind of class he has. He said,
'You know if you go with me, a lot of people will attribute
things you do later as a coach to our relationship.' Well, Dean
had already had a tremendous influence on my thinking, but
this was just an example of his honesty. He was trying to
make me aware that when I worked with him, there was the
possibility of people saying I learned this or that from Dean
Smith, rather than giving me credit for being able to think and
function.

"I have been a disciple of Dean for years, though. I think it's
a sign of intelligence to learn from others. Who was it, Emer-
son, who said genius borrows nobly? I think of myself as
being reasonably intelligent, and I think of Dean as probably
one of the most learned men in the game of basketball. So I
have absolutely no problem in trying to copy or do anything
that he does, because I think anyone who does is copying
from the best."

In attempting to put a finger on Smith's most outstanding
feature as a coach, Thompson said, "It's his organizational
mind, as far as I'm concerned. I mean, particularly as it relates
to the game. For example, you start to talk to Dean Smith

John Thompson

about time-outs, and he can almost show you the way his are structured. He starts talking about his four corners or his fast break, and it's the same way. The man's mind runs organized; he puts order into the game. There is order in his manner of teaching, besides the fact that he has introduced so many concepts in relation to the passing game, the four corners, and other things. He's that way about most things. Look at his meticulous manner of dressing. I kid him a lot and even laugh when I hear him order in a restaurant. Everything is organized. It's just natural for him."

Thompson commented on the tendency of some people to characterize Smith's clean image as phony or pretentious. "These things others say are a sign of success. I think you should become a little worried if people don't talk about you, particularly in this profession. But Dean Smith exemplifies that old expression Flip Wilson used, 'What you see is what you get.' At least that's my personal opinion. I don't think Dean is pretentious at all. A lot of times, coaches may be very critical of people like Dean when they see the cohesiveness he has in his program, because things he has are things all coaches want in their own teams. If Dean Smith is a phony, then everyone should be a phony, because Dean has had a tremendous amount of success. His kids respect him, his kids graduate from school, and his kids play professional basketball. He has genuine concern for his kids, and that's one of the things which has earned my respect for the man. The relationship I have observed that he has with his players is the thing, especially a player who has experienced a certain difficulty. I have seen Dean spend an inordinate amount of time trying to help a player, even when it did not behoove him to do anything for the player. Still, he would try to get the kid headed in the right direction. That impressed me because Dean had nothing to gain, and what he did never became public knowledge. He does things like that and never tells anyone about it."

Thompson was in a unique position when he was a high

school coach at St. Anthony's in Washington, D.C. His highly recruited star player, Donald Washington, eventually chose to attend North Carolina. Thompson was also Washington's legal guardian. "I have had the good fortune of dealing with Dean from the standpoint of a coach, a parent, and also as an assistant to him," Thompson said. "So I know the man from firsthand experience. He can communicate as well as carry out the technical aspects of coaching, and his basic ingredient in his communication is honesty. He deals with those things a person wants to hear and those a person doesn't want to hear. He is very open and honest with his players and with those he is recruiting. His players know where they stand; he'll let a player know before a game starts exactly how he plans on using him. A lot of coaches keep players in doubt because they don't want to deal with that type of thing. Dean will sit down and tell a player he is going to come in for this other player, or he'll tell another player what his role is. Sometimes there is a lot of difficulty in doing this, but I think Dean's willingness to handle it gets very positive results. A lot of coaches tell people only what they want to hear in order to get what they want, but Dean is not going to say something if it interferes with his philosophy. He can deal with conflict as well as positive situations. He has rapport with his players, and a lot of it comes from his straightforwardness.

"Dean is very flexible, which is a great asset. The fact that he was known for so long for his four corners, yet his teams have been running teams, is a perfect example. He has a lot of versatility within himself; his range of knowledge is vast.

"It's difficult for me to express my feelings for Dean. I feel he works very hard at being a decent person. Now, I don't mean he tries to do what people will think is good. No, he works hard at doing things all people should do. He cares about other people. I don't think he is a god, but he is as consistent as anybody I've met—consistent in his personality and feelings for others. I often tell my friends that Dean has been as honest and open about the coaching trade as he can be. It's a little, intangible thing about this business which doesn't just relate to the X's and O's of the game. He has shared himself with me. A lot of people give you things, but very few tell you things so that you can help yourself. Dean Smith has, and I think he has tried to help many other coaches. It's hard to find folks who will share the fruits of their experiences with you in order to try and protect you from some of the things they have encountered. He's done that with me."

Mike Krzyzewski

Mike Krzyzewski has built one of the country's strongest basketball programs at Duke. His teams have been regular visitors to the Final Four in recent years, and he has consistently graduated all of his players. His relationship with Smith is an interesting one, in that Duke is an archrival of North Carolina's, with the campuses only eight miles apart. Krzyzewski played for Bobby Knight at Army before serving as Knight's assistant.

"Even before I started coaching at Duke, I had the utmost respect for Dean and what he had accomplished," Krzyzewski said. "Being around Coach Knight, I knew people who had established themselves in college basketball. Dean was and is one of those people. You have to be around a long time to accomplish what Dean has. Being in the ACC and seeing what he's done, I have even more respect for him now. Having competed against him, I know how well he prepares his teams, how well he teaches them, and how well he handles situations in games."

Krzyzewski also spoke of what Smith does away from the basketball arena. "I have more respect for Dean behind the scenes," the Duke coach said. "He serves on committees to improve basketball; he has worked very hard in this area. And he does a lot for the community, for the state of North Carolina. What he puts back into the area and state is signifi-

Mike Krzyzewski

cant. And he does it right. His players go to class and graduate, and there is never any question about his sticking to the rules in recruiting."

Because of the Duke-Carolina rivalry, Smith and Krzyzewski are perceived by many people to be enemies. After all, that's what is expected from archrivals. There isn't any truth in that perception, though. "I really like Dean," Krzyzewski said. "I know there are no corners cut where he and his program are concerned. I like discussing things with him. The man has been in college basketball a long time and has worked to improve it. I enjoy hearing what he has to say; it's interesting to talk with him. Unfortunately, because of the intense nature of our schools' rivalry, it isn't possible to spend a lot of time with the coach from North Carolina. But the time I do spend is enjoyable. We have our different styles. We do things differently. But Duke and Carolina both do things the right way. We win and our kids get degrees. The really good programs don't need other programs to do badly in order to be uplifted. Duke and Carolina consistently have success, and there is room for that. I don't consider Dean an enemy. I admire him."

As for Smith's long-running hit show in Chapel Hill, Krzyzewski said, "A lot of people can do it for one year, or they can build a program when it's down. Few can sustain. Dean has sustained excellence. When you talk about the man, you're talking about success in the sixties, seventies, and eighties. Now he's doing it in the nineties. He's an institution."

The Duke coach feels Smith's experience and expertise should be called upon more by the NCAA. "Not many know what the heck went on in the sixties," Krzyzewski said. "Well, when you have somebody with the knowledge and background of Dean, you want to listen to him. You would ask somebody like that about his opinion on issues. He is worth listening to; so is Coach Knight. You're foolish if you don't listen to people like Dean and Coach Knight."

Krzyzewski is as fierce a competitor as Smith. Their rivalry has been heated, and their teams' confrontations have produced some classics. "I don't know if I'd call our rivalry fun," Krzyzewski said. "It is certainly intense. And it has made me a better coach. You know there is no downside anywhere with Dean; he'll be prepared. As a result, I have to be totally prepared, too. He forces you to be at your best. The competition has brought a very high level of play into our program.

"I respect what Dean does. He's a Hall of Famer. He has done a great deal for the game of basketball. He has just contributed so much. I admire that. He has been consistently great."

Frank McGuire

Frank McGuire brought Dean Smith to Chapel Hill as his assistant in 1958, a year after North Carolina posted a 32–0 record, won the national championship, and earned McGuire the national coach-of-the-year award. He had received the same honor earlier in his career at St. John's. After leaving the Tar Heels, McGuire coached in the NBA, then returned to the collegiate scene to serve as South Carolina coach from 1964 to 1980. He is a member of the National Basketball Hall of Fame.

McGuire has sung Smith's praises from the time he hired Smith as an assistant, and he continues to be one of the North Carolina coach's most vocal supporters. "I think Dean will go down as one of the greatest coaches in history," McGuire said. "Right now, he rates probably the highest among today's coaches, but he didn't just fall into that distinction. He has worked hard. He always keeps trying to better himself. His inventiveness is what he is best known for, but Dean doesn't just have the intelligence to think of new things; he has the good sense to know how to use them, and he is not afraid to stick by his ideas. Take that game when his team trailed 7–0 at the half at Duke [in the final game of the 1978–79 regular season]. I'll tell anyone, that took nerve. Not that

Frank McGuire

many coaches would have that kind of nerve—to stick with what they thought was best when it was such an unpopular decision. But that's the way Dean is. He's not going to worry about what people think. He isn't afraid of criticism. He's going to stick by his guns."

McGuire spoke about the envy opposing schools' fans sometimes feel because of Carolina's success. "I was on a talk show out of a radio station in Raleigh, North Carolina, and this man called in and asked me why people hate Dean Smith so much. I said, 'That's an easy one—Dean beats their teams.' Coaches are disliked for two reasons: they either lose too much or win too much. It's the greatest compliment in the world to say everyone dislikes Dean, although everyone doesn't—just a lot of folks who root for teams other than North Carolina."

McGuire cited recruiting and the closeness of Smith's teams as two of the reasons why the Tar Heels have fared so well for so long. "Dean recruits players who fit into his mold. He could have a lot of others that he doesn't even go after. There was Mike O'Koren. At South Carolina, I would have played him the whole game, and he would have scored 35 or 40 points a game. But Dean has more players. Mike would do whatever Dean asked, and so will the other North Carolina players. They believe in Dean. A coach has to have that to succeed. Look at Phil Ford when he was playing. He was a great one-on-one player, but he'd do anything Dean asked of him. Same with Walter Davis. They went on to be the same way in the pros, too. No one ever hears of anyone having trouble with any of Dean's players. They have sacrificed in college and will in the pros. Ford went into the stands after the ball. Mitch Kupchak got on the floor after the ball and hurt himself at times. And Walter Davis plays totally for his team. They all play for the team; that's what Dean coaches. The way his guys go to the pros and play, and the fact that they are such fine young men—those things are great compliments to their college coach.

"I love to watch Dean's teams play. They have that great enthusiasm, and Dean has great enthusiasm, too. I'd hate to attend one of North Carolina's games and sit behind the Tar Heel bench. I would never see any of the game, because the players are always up and cheering one another. Dean has the ability to keep all of his players happy. They stick together and are happy with whatever role he gives them. But they are a certain type of kid; they have to be to adjust to his coaching. He goes after that certain type of kid. . . .

"Sure, he has the players," McGuire said. "He gets great players, but it's what he does with those players that is the mark of his outstanding coaching ability. Many coaches get great players but can't win. Not like Dean does. Look at his ACC record.

"I saw a great career coming for Dean because he wasn't afraid to work; he studies and tries to improve, and he tries different things. He pays attention to everything. It was rough for him at first, especially with us having won the national championship in 1957. I imagine when Dean loses his first game every year, there is still someone who will compare Dean and his team to the one I had that year when we won them all. It's tougher than ever now, though. There are better athletes, and it's not as easy to dominate. I was so happy when he won the national championship in '82. But he was a great, great coach before that."

McGuire feels that Smith's NCAA title is not the greatest testimony to his coaching prowess. "No, having a place named for you is much, much bigger," said the man who gave Smith his chance in Chapel Hill. "The Smith Center is marvelous, and it's quite an honor for Dean that it was named for him. It's only fitting, though; he deserves it. People would have gone crazy if it had been named anything else.

"I love Dean and continue to keep up with him. Everything he has received, he has earned. He is brilliant."

Dave Gavitt

Dave Gavitt served the last 10 years of his 18-year coaching career at Providence College, then retired from coaching at the end of the 1978–79 season to serve as that school's athletic director. He was the commissioner of the Big East Conference for 11 years, from the time of that league's inception. He is now director of operations for the Boston Celtics.

"Dean and I have become close friends over the years," Gavitt said. "I have found him to be a very, very bright, articulate, and concerned person. I think a large part of his coaching success has come because he has such great depth of personality and character. And I really believe Dean Smith would have been successful in anything he might have chosen to do, even something other than coaching basketball. I think his ability to have the kind of unique insight and to use his intelligence, coupled with his exceptional ability to motivate young people, has made him an outstanding coach.

"For a while, there was some criticism because Dean had not won a national title. I've always said the difficult thing about the NCAA Tournament is getting there; and once you're there, almost anything can happen. He has gotten there often. I don't think coaches, as a whole, put all that much stock in national championships. There are other things—like the ability to teach, having your players graduate, and having integrity—that are more important. Dean has all that. His national reputation is the finest."

Gavitt and Smith have worked together on a number of projects. "Our relationship has been a close one," Gavitt said. "We have had quite a bit of association in international basketball, and we both became involved in the Olympic movement. We worked closely on various committees and in the selection processes involved in choosing the players to represent the United States in international competition. We have also served together on the board of directors of the National Association of Basketball Coaches and have helped with numer-

Dave Gavitt

ous clinics here and in foreign countries. I think Dean has been a tremendous representative of the college game in almost every way, in terms of public relations and in terms of his study of the rules. I think if I were a university president, I couldn't conceive of anyone I'd rather have representing our school.

"It's difficult to pinpoint any one thing as the biggest or best contribution Dean has made to college basketball. He is very innovative in the things he's done, and he has had a tremendous impact on the international scene of basketball. He has done so much."

Bob Weinhauer

Bob Weinhauer is the director of player personnel and chief scout for the Philadelphia 76ers of the NBA. Prior to taking that job, he established himself as a fine college coach, guiding University of Pennsylvania teams into the NCAA Tournament in 1978 and 1979. In 1979, he took the Quakers to the Final Four, and they knocked off North Carolina along the way. Ironically, prior to the 1978–79 season, Weinhauer visited Smith and his Tar Heels. Here, he reflects upon that experience.

"Coach Smith had been nice enough to allow me to visit and observe North Carolina's practice during the first few days of his team's drills," Weinhauer said. "He allowed me to sit in the stands and watch the practices, and then he went so far as to let me sit in on the coaches' meetings. I actually talked with Dean and went over the films with him—things like that. We weren't just looking at the North Carolina system, but were talking basketball in general. That was a wonderful opportunity.

"Having visited with Dean like I did, beating his team did not give me as great a feeling of elation as it might have. When you beat a very good team, particularly a very well-coached team, there is a certain amount of satisfaction that

Bob Weinhauer

goes with that victory. I was a high school coach for 12 years, and I had respected Dean Smith all the way through my coaching career. It was enough of a thrill for me just to have my team play against one of his teams, but to be so fortunate as to win that game just made it a little something extra. To win, though, was not necessary to enjoy that feeling of competing against him. We were playing one of the great people of the game. . . .

"There has always been a great exchange of thoughts between and among coaches," Weinhauer said. "They are all trying to improve themselves. I certainly was not the first or only coach to go to Dean Smith's practices. He happens to be one of the top men in the profession, and if you're going to observe someone, you want to go to the top. That's what I felt I was doing. Aside from running probably the best practice I've ever seen, Dean is a first-class gentleman and person.

"From the standpoint of what Dean's teams actually get done in a practice, what they accomplish on the floor, and from the standpoint of the rapport between the coaching staff and the players, it is just a highly organized situation. Of course, we can say that all coaches are well organized, but Dean's practices were something special to me. There was something there a coach could not have if it was his first year of coaching, something that has to build up—a respect between the coach and his players, a respect for the coach's program which has to build over a period of years. That's what they have at North Carolina. It's an intangible type of respect, and one can see it in the way the players there perform in practice and in games."

Weinhauer offered a few reasons why Smith has been so successful. "First is his relationship with his players—the tremendous amount of respect they have for him and what he has been able to accomplish at North Carolina. Second is his organizational ability; Dean is just so thorough. And then he is an innovator. Not every coach is, but Dean comes up with new ideas and very good ones. He is one of the great coaches."

Bobby Knight

Although his personality and on-court demeanor are quite different from Dean Smith's, Indiana Coach Bobby Knight is very much like his North Carolina counterpart in other regards. Like Smith, Knight is an outstanding teacher of basketball. He insists that his players be good students, and a very high percentage of them receive degrees. Also like Smith, Knight played on an NCAA championship team (at Ohio State), coached a team to the national title (three Hoosier teams, actually), and guided a United States Olympic team to a gold medal (in Los Angeles in 1984).

"Dean and I have been good friends since I first started coaching at Army, which was shortly after he began at North Carolina," Knight said. "We have tried to do things the right way, and our basic approach to the things that are important in the game of basketball is very similar.

"Dean and I have talked a lot over the years about various aspects of college basketball, both on and off the court. I have always enjoyed the games that we at Indiana have played with North Carolina because I know I can be very pleased with the kids representing both schools, regardless of who wins."

Knight and Smith have shared basketball strategies. "I have really enjoyed our talks and my friendship with Dean over the years," Knight said. "I consider him an enjoyable person to be around and one that I can enjoy talking to about a lot of things other than basketball.

"Dean has a tremendous grasp of the game at both ends of the court, and this is the basis of what I think is his most significant contribution to the game of basketball. That is the total approach a coach must have in the development of a team."

Bobby Knight

Bill Guthridge

Bill Guthridge is Smith's chief assistant coach at North Carolina. He has been on the Tar Heel staff for 23 years. Guthridge works with both the offensive and defensive schemes and is also Carolina's shooting instructor. He was invited to coach the Puerto Rican team in the 1968 Olympics, but he declined because of his work at Carolina. He assisted Smith with the 1976 United States Olympic team.

Guthridge carries an outstanding reputation. He has turned down numerous head-coaching jobs across the nation while withdrawing his name from consideration for several others. Part of the reason is his close relationship with Smith. "I think I have chosen not to be a head coach," Guthridge said. "I don't know of many jobs I'd rather have than the one I have now, but the main reason I don't want to leave Carolina is Coach Smith. I think it's obvious he is the best coach in the college game."

In attempting to pinpoint Smith's greatest strength as a coach, Guthridge said, "There are so many. He is very intelligent not just about basketball; he is a highly intelligent man. But maybe the main thing is that he understands people so well. He seems to be able to anticipate some problems that people are going to have. And this, of course, helps in being a coach and in working with young men. It's amazing to me the time he puts in with people and the things he does for people. He spends an unbelievable amount of time helping former players, and every year there are two, three, or four more added to the list. And he'll do whatever he can for any of his former players.

"It's just something the way he'll take so much time with the press. Like after a heartbreaking loss, Coach Smith will go out and answer all the writers' questions, although he may not feel like it. He will stand there and keep answering questions, some of which have been asked over and over and some of which are really ridiculous anyway. He has patience."

Bill Guthridge

Much has been said about Smith's treatment of his players, and Guthridge has been right there to witness it for more than two decades. "The Mike O'Korens and Phil Fords aren't treated any differently from the Eric Kennys, Ged Doughtons, and Mickey Bells," Guthridge said. "Coach Smith makes every player feel very important. He does a great job at that because they are all important to him. He gives every player a fair chance. Then he assigns roles, and every player has a valuable contribution to make. It's unbelievable the number of hours Coach Smith has put in for Ford, Bobby Jones, Bob McAdoo, Walter Davis, Michael Jordan, James Worthy, and Kenny Smith, but also for Doughton, Randy Wiel, Jeff Denny, and others. He feels one of his major responsibilities is to make sure seniors get situated and get the job they want. He'll set up interviews and counsel the players. Coach Smith helped the guys in pro ball make a lot of money. They might have had lawyers, but Coach knows what's going on and works with the lawyers. He always asks the real good players if they want to go hardship before they are seniors, and he feels very strongly that they should do what they want. Coach Smith feels some people attend college to obtain financial security, and if a player chooses to make a lot of money by leaving here early, then he'll help the player do just that. He doesn't take into consideration that North Carolina could have a better team if the player stayed."

Guthridge has known Smith 38 years, dating back to the time their paths crossed in Kansas. When he was in high school in Parsons, Guthridge met Smith through his sister, Joan, who was dating the future Carolina coach at the time. "I was always impressed by him, even from the first time I came to Chapel Hill. When I got here, I was shocked and amazed at some of the things he was able to do with the team both on and off the court. The way he treated me was an example of the kind of person he is. I remember once when my sister, her husband and family, [and] my mother came to visit me at Chapel Hill for the first time. Well, Coach Smith took the whole day just to show them around like he was recruiting them. I knew he had a lot of other things to do, and yet he did that."

Guthridge touched on Smith's organizational ability and his flexibility. "He is a very good organizer, but he is also very good at making adjustments. He can make quick adjustments; he knows you can't plan out a whole life or a whole season, so he has a great knack for changing when he has to change. He plans, though, and he plans for everything. His last-minute situation preparation is an example. Like that 17-second comeback with Duke—that wasn't something that just happened. That was something we had rehearsed for years—how to stop the other team from getting the ball inbounds, when to foul, how to get the ball in ourselves, and how to get the ball to a certain player for certain shots. We worked on those situations every practice for years, day in and day out. We start on the first day of practice every year, October 15, working on last-minute situations, and we work on some type of late-game situations every day."

Guthridge spoke of Smith's personality and the effect it has on the Carolina team. "Coach is very composed on game day, very much in control of himself. I've never seen him lose control of himself, and this radiates to the team. He has poise, and I think our teams reflect the same kind of emotion. Coach Smith gets technical fouls, of course, but he has control of himself.

"If anyone was to ask in the coaching profession who is the most copied and respected basketball coach, it would be far and away Coach Smith. If the question were asked, 'Which program would you love to have your program be like?' North Carolina would be the most frequent answer. It's because of the number of players who graduate, the number of players who go on to the pros, the team morale—the way our players stand up on the bench and cheer. Coach Smith is the reason for all of these things. I've heard it said Coach puts up a facade, but I know him, and believe me, there is nothing phony about him. He's a Christian, he lives by Christian ethics, and he is very easy to work with."

Looking back on Smith's accomplishments, Guthridge found it impossible to single out one as the Tar Heel coach's most distinguished. "It's astounding to me what he's done and how he's done it," Guthridge said. "There are several things which stand out to me. One is his coming in like he did after Frank McGuire. A coach who follows another extremely successful coach often doesn't last even with good conditions. Coach Smith had bad conditions he had to survive. Then, to weather the early storm and get back—that was something. He got Bob Lewis, Larry Miller, and the five guys [Rusty Clark, Dick Grubar, Bill Bunting, Gerald Tuttle, and Joe Brown] together, then Charlie Scott. After three ACC championships, we were 18–9, then were voted by some to finish last in the league. We won the regular season and the NIT instead. We came back and won the ACC Tournament when we weren't supposed to during David Thompson's senior year at N.C. State. In 1979, it looked like we really weren't supposed to be good, and we tied for the regular-season championship and won the tourney. And of course the eighties meant more success, including the national championship. Those were the key things—consistency and the ability to have big years when they didn't look likely.

"Coach Smith has had his innovations—some great ones— but one asset which is unique is his ability to take whatever happens and make something positive out of it. Working with him has been a wonderful experience."

Lefty Driesell

Over the years, Lefty Driesell has seen Dean Smith operate frequently. While building solid programs at Davidson, Maryland, and now James Madison, Driesell has sent his teams in

Lefty Driesell

against Smith's North Carolina Tar Heels over 40 times. During a short stint out of coaching, the Lefthander also studied Smith and his teams as a television color commentator.

"I wouldn't say we always got along," Driesell said of his relationship with Smith. "We had some misunderstandings at [ACC] coaches' meetings. But I've always respected Dean as a man and as a coach.

"He knows the game of basketball and is a good teacher. I watched his practices when I was an announcer, and I saw just how intense Dean is. I could tell he wants to win bad; he got on those boys pretty hard. People don't think he does, but he's not easy. I've certainly seen guys who are more laid-back in practice than Dean is.

"When you're a competitor with someone, you don't go around and visit him in his office," Driesell said. "When I was an announcer, Dean took me around, and I got to know him. My first one-on-one interview on TV was with him, and I remember that he bailed me out. He kind of took over so that I didn't have to ask a lot of questions; he made it easy. Interviews are the toughest things to do, and I was nervous. Dean was wanting me to do well, and he was very helpful. I'll always remember that.

"But he is always cooperative and helpful with the press," Driesell said. "He's great at public relations. He is also an excellent coach. In our profession, you look at how many a guy has won and how many he has lost. Dean's record tells how good he is. He has had great players, and he has taken those players and molded them into teams that play together well. He has had great tradition, but he has been able to maintain it and keep it at Carolina. That's harder to do than to just build it. He has never really had a dry spell.

"To say that he's slipping is ridiculous. Every time Carolina loses a game or two, folks say stuff like that, and it's ludicrous. Dean is in a situation any coach is in when he's been at a place for a while—people take him for granted. They say he hasn't won a championship since Michael Jordan left, or they say this or that. If you win one, though, you've done more than 99 percent of the coaches in the country. Dean has been at North Carolina so long that people don't appreciate him.

"They should, though."

Roy Williams

After spending 10 years on Dean Smith's North Carolina coaching staff, Roy Williams landed the head-coaching job at Kansas University following the departure of Larry Brown to the NBA's San Antonio Spurs. A longtime Smith disciple, Williams immediately earned a reputation of his own, thanks to his outstanding record with the Jayhawks.

"Here I am, the head basketball coach at Kansas," Williams said, "and there's no way that Roy Williams is the head basketball coach at Kansas without Dean Smith. That's a pretty obvious statement, to say the least. I am very fortunate to have spent 10 years as his assistant.

"The day after Larry Brown left Kansas, the athletic director from that school called Coach Smith, and he did the wise thing in asking Coach Smith to take the job. Coach said he wouldn't do that, but they started talking about other coaches, and Coach Smith threw out my name. I was going out the door [of the UNC basketball office] and Coach Smith said he had been talking with the Kansas A.D. and that he thought I had a chance. I didn't even believe it. There were a lot of people out there who wanted that job, but because of Coach Smith's influence and the way he is respected throughout the country—particularly here at Kansas, his alma mater—I was given consideration and got the job. There was no way I was going to get it without Dean Smith."

As for the aspects of Smith's coaching that have made an impact on his own career, Williams said, "The first thing that jumps out is his organization. He feels you've got to have a plan, a game plan, a master plan. It involves the dormitory,

Roy Williams

study hall, training table, games, practice, conditioning, everything. Along with that, he has the understanding that it is a group of individuals that you're trying to get to play a team game. But he doesn't lose sight of the fact that you're working with 20-year-old youngsters, and the work that you do with the kids is more important than the result of the games. He believes that. To him, it's not just the wins and losses. Now, that's important, but not the most important. Doing the best you can is what matters most.

"I never saw Coach Smith angry after a loss," Williams said. "I've seen him frustrated. It was always amazing to me that after a loss, he would say we needed to do a better job of coaching; he never put the blame on the kids. And he's not going to do that. The maddest you'll ever see Dean Smith is when there is a lack of effort during practice. He doesn't go into an uncontrolled rage then, but he's got that part of him that doesn't like less than a 100-percent effort."

As for Smith the person, Williams said, "The way he has touched people's lives—everybody that he's come in contact with—is just phenomenal. Coach Smith does more things for people without anyone ever knowing about it than most people do and want credit for it. I think he's the best coach there is, but he is even better off the court—the way he cares for people. The people who work and play for him don't just work and play for him; they get a part of him. That, to me, is his greatest strength."

Williams reflected upon his friendship with Smith. "I've been a very, very lucky man," he said. "When we had a pretty good season my first year at Kansas, someone asked me how did what I accomplished compare to Dean Smith. Well, when people compare anybody to Dean Smith, they're not doing the other person justice. There are a lot of guys who won a lot of basketball games, but there's nobody . . . who has the total package like he does—winning the games, graduating the kids, doing what is best for the kids, representing the university the way it should be done, being an example of the way things should be in college athletics. There's nobody who has the package like he does.

"I guess the best thing about me as a coach is that I've been exposed to the best teacher there is."

Eddie Fogler

Like Roy Williams, Eddie Fogler is a former Smith assistant, having served on the North Carolina staff for 13 years before becoming Wichita State's head basketball coach. From there, he moved to his present position as head coach at Vanderbilt. Fogler also played as a guard on Smith's teams in the late sixties, helping the Tar Heels win two ACC championships.

"Dean Smith is not your everyday person," Fogler said. "He is very easygoing, and very little bothers him. I've never seen him snap at anyone. God made just one like him. I could take a week telling the things about him which impress me, but to say it briefly, I'd just say the man is all class.

"He is a man at the top of his profession. If someone wants to study law, he goes to Harvard; if anyone wants to be a pro basketball player, he should go to North Carolina. Dean Smith is the professor of basketball. Playing for him is like taking a four-year course in basketball. A player learns the fundamentals, learns how to play defense, and just learns the entire game under Coach Smith."

Smith is known as a selective recruiter, one who goes after certain players he feels will fit into his system and who will be good students. There have been times when a bit more stroking of high school stars' egos might have meant big catches for UNC, but Smith doesn't play that game. "Coach is so honest," Fogler said. "In fact, he has lost players he was recruiting because of his honesty. He doesn't want to mislead them. I've heard him tell kids he doesn't think they will play very much for the first two years; he won't promise anything. As a result, no one goes to Carolina not knowing where he stands."

It has been said that players with great talents don't have

Eddie Fogler

the opportunity to realize their full offensive potential under Smith. "What I say to that," Fogler remarked, "is first, that Dean Smith believes basketball is a team game. It is not a one-man show. Second, I'd say look where the players are in the NBA; Coach Smith makes his players better players. Third, ask the players. I mean, it's no coincidence Michael Jordan was the NBA defensive player of the year. He learned how to guard people. Now, how many coaches in the country are going to make Michael Jordan learn to play defense?"

Fogler discussed Smith's influence on his life, saying, "Each year, I refer back to something Coach Smith said or something he taught me in terms of making decisions, in terms of my profession, or in terms of my personal life. He's always there in that respect. My teams do a lot of the same things as Coach Smith's. At least we try. We try from an X-and-O standpoint to do a lot of what North Carolina does, but I just don't teach it as well.

"As a coach, he gets quality people to adhere to a quality philosophy in terms of the student-athlete concept and life after basketball. And those kids win games. Coach Smith has shown that. Certainly, they have had great players like Michael Jordan, but they have also had a bunch of overachievers who have helped win a lot of games for North Carolina. That is a tribute to the coach.

"You know, I'm not so sure down the road, whenever Coach Smith decides to hang 'em up, and you sit back and put it all on a piece of paper—it'll take a lot of pieces of paper—and you evaluate what his coaching career has done in terms of wins and losses, graduation rate, where his players are today—and all within the rules—it will be awesome. Absolutely awesome! I know people appreciate what he has done, but I'm not sure until Coach Smith has retired and everybody looks at it will they realize just how amazing it all is. Also, that it is never going to be done again.

"There is nobody who is going to run the total-package program and win as many games in [the ACC] as Coach Smith has."

INSIDE DEAN SMITH

Beneath the well-dressed exterior, Dean Smith is much like everyone else. He has far more to do than is possible in a 24-hour day. He is aware of the world's excess of people and its shortage of just about everything else. He experiences frustrations. He does not pretend to live within the boundaries of a basketball court. Smith is a loving husband and father. He engages in outside interests, but unlike many persons, his greatest joy is his profession. Because of his heavy involvement in coaching-related activities, he has very little leisure time.

College basketball coaches stay relatively busy with their basic responsibilities. There are at least 30 games per season, including preseason exhibitions and postseason tournaments. There are practice sessions from October through March, recruiting trips, coaching staff meetings, summer camps, and radio and television shows.

For Smith, there are countless other duties as well, some of them self-imposed. His interest in more than 175 former players saps much of his time, though it is not spent grudgingly. There are a multitude of clinics and speaking engagements. And service to organizations like the Fellowship of Christian Athletes, the National Association of Basketball Coaches, the National Basketball Hall of Fame, the NCAA Select Committee, and various Olympic committees requires many long hours.

Smith has received the prestigious Golden Plate Award from the American Academy of Achievement. The only other coaches to have won the award are John Wooden, Bud Wilkinson, Bear Bryant, Joe Paterno, and Tom Landry. Smith was also presented the Distinguished Service Citation by his alma mater, Kansas University. It is the highest honor that university can bestow upon an individual to acknowledge outstanding accomplishments for the betterment of society.

One example of Smith's broad interest in social justice came in 1960, when he and his pastor at Binkley Baptist Church, the Reverend Bob Seymour, had dinner with a black man at one of Chapel Hill's more prominent, yet segregated, restaurants. The story has been exaggerated over the years—one version has it that Smith and his party sat at a downtown lunch counter. "Actually, it was a quiet, uneventful meal," Seymour said. "We were admitted and served. The fact that Dean made a statement, that he took a stand, is what is important. When someone like him does something like that, people take notice.

"It was part of a concerted effort by the Christian community to try to open some doors which were closed," Seymour said. "Chapel Hill was thought of as a liberal kind of community, but in matters of race, it was as Southern as any town anywhere. Other people were involved, but no one the stature of Dean. He was very much committed to opening restaurants and other places to all colors."

Seymour recalled another issue on which Smith took a stand. "In the eighties, he went public in calling for a nuclear

Carolina's Final Top-10
National Rankings under Dean Smith

Year	AP	UPI
1966-67	3rd	4th
1967-68	4th	3rd
1968-69	4th	2nd
1971-72	2nd	2nd
1973-74	—	8th
1974-75	9th	10th
1975-76	8th	6th
1976-77	5th	3rd
1977-78	—	10th
1978-79	9th	3rd
1980-81	6th	6th
1981-82	1st	1st
1982-83	8th	8th
1983-84	1st	1st
1984-85	7th	7th
1985-86	8th	8th
1986-87	2nd	3rd
1987-88	7th	8th
1988-89	5th	4th

Other Appearances for UNC in the Top 20

Year	AP	UPI
1970-71	13th	13th
1972-73	11th	12th
1979-80	15th	15th

All-Time Top-10 Poll Finishes (AP or UPI) by Coach

1. Dean Smith, North Carolina 19
2. Adolph Rupp, Kentucky 18
3. John Wooden, UCLA 13
4. Lefty Driesell, Davidson and Maryland 9
   Bobby Knight, Indiana 9
   Al McGuire, Marquette 9
   Jerry Tarkanian, UNLV and Long Beach State 9
8. Digger Phelps, Notre Dame...8

freeze. Dean does a lot of things quietly, but this was one of the few times he has publicly supported an issue of that kind. The matter of a freeze triggered some backlash; some people were pretty upset about it. Because they didn't share Dean's view, they felt he shouldn't have said anything."

Seymour first knew Smith as a church member and friend, not as a basketball coach. "I came to Chapel Hill caring nothing about basketball," Seymour said. "Dean would say to me that one of the things he liked about me was that I was one of the few people in his life who didn't want to talk basketball.

"Dean is very generous, and he always wants to give credit to other people. I saw him as being very uncomfortable talking about himself. He taught a Sunday school class and was a deacon in our church. That was early in his career. Whenever there was any cause that he was aware of, Dean would say he wanted to be a part of it. When there was a need for money, he would be very generous—with the stipulation that no one knew of his involvement. He has been a consistent and strong supporter of Binkley Baptist Church for 30 years."

Seymour sees the North Carolina coach as a man somewhat trapped by his celebrity status. "I think it's been tough in that everyone wants a piece of Dean," Seymour said. "I don't think he likes being called a private person, but being a celebrity, he almost has to be private. He does have a few restaurants, though, where he goes and hides; no one knows he's there. He likes that."

Smith is the father of five children, three by his first wife, Ann, and two by his wife of 14 years, Linnea. Sharon Kepley, his oldest child, was born in March 1955. She graduated from the University of North Carolina in 1977 with a Bachelor of Arts degree in psychology. She is the director of a day-care center in Chapel Hill, where she and her husband, Tim, reside with their daughter, Megan, and son, Drew. Sandy Smith was born in September 1956 and graduated from UNC in 1978 with a Bachelor of Arts degree in history. She received her master's degree in education counseling at the University of

Kelly and Kristen Smith

Virginia and is now with National Bank of Washington, D.C. Smith's son, Scott, was born in June 1958 and graduated from North Carolina in 1980 with a double major in liberal arts and physical education. He is a representative of the Converse Shoe Company and resides in Chapel Hill with his wife, Kelli. Smith's youngest children are Kristen, born in March 1979, and Kelly, born in February 1981.

Smith spoke of the end of his first marriage."The divorce was the most traumatic thing I have ever been through," he said. "It wasn't an arguing thing or anything like that; it was just difficult. I told the kids that I was moving out, and I roomed with John Lotz [then an assistant to Smith] for a while, then went back home and tried it for another year. It just didn't work. Everything has all worked out now, though, as far as the children and I are concerned, and I hope for Ann, too."

Smith and Linnea married in May 1976. She is a medical doctor with a specialty in psychiatry. She and Dean spend more time discussing psychology and Christian theology than they do basketball. "Linnea goes to our home games and some of the away games," Smith said, "but she had never been very interested in basketball before she met me. She enjoys the games, but she doesn't go up and down emo tionally in relation to how our team is doing. She gets down a little bit if we lose, but not as much as a player or coach.

"The kids have shown a big interest in basketball, with Scott more involved than the girls. Sharon and Sandy have great interest, but when we lose, they aren't crushed. Scott is." Just as Smith once asked questions of his father following games, so did Scott when he was growing up. "He might have thrown out something like, 'Why did you do that?'" Smith said. "He has always felt bad after Carolina loses, and I try to tell him he shouldn't feel that way. There has not been a lot of discussion about basketball at home; I have tried to avoid that. If I have work to do, I go do it—perhaps talking on the phone or watching films in the study. Scott and I may have discussed offense or defense when he was at home, but I didn't replay games there."

Some of Smith's deepest interests have come from his family. It was his sister, Joan, who helped stimulate his appetite for theology, and books on that subject dominated Smith's reading for years. "I read very few novels," he said. "John Updike was about the only author whose novels I would read." Smith became extremely well read in theology, though, with Paul Tillich, Paul Tournier, Elton Trueblood, Sören Kierkegaard, Dietrich Bonhoeffer, Waldo Beach, Sam Hill, Leslie Weatherhead, and C. S. Lewis among the authors who helped shape his own ideas.

"I believe Christian faith is motivated by gratitude," Smith said, "not for material things, obviously, but for love and acceptance. It's the acceptance of a person as himself. I don't think we are built this way; we're more selfish by human nature. Therefore, if we are still loved and accepted, perhaps we'll be more caring and accepting toward others. . . . One could say the story of the prodigal son is the theme of the New Testament, as I understand it. I'm sure that the son who came back was so grateful that he might have responded in ethical action. To reach that point of gratitude, there first has to come a need, and some people never really come to a point of need to discover this acceptance. I do believe there was a person, Jesus of Nazareth. I think He did live and die and rise again. I believe in the Resurrection. I realize Paul said that's why there is the whole Christian faith, and that's why we're still talking about it 2,000 years later. But I do not believe in Christ dying for people. I think He was a man who lived a perfect life and was crucified through people's choices, and God would work most perfectly through Him. I don't believe a loving God would sacrifice someone; I can't believe in the hell idea for the same reason. . . .

"I'm against the merit system; I believe we are saved or accepted regardless of our attitude and good works. I know I am happier when I'm not thinking so selfishly. I don't think that there are just a few full-time Christian-service vocations. I think coaching can be a full-time Christian service, or anything else can for that matter. I remember being so caught up in the thought that there were certain careers like this that once in the eighth grade, I prayed to get a base hit in a baseball game and promised God that if I got the hit, I would be a medical missionary. I got the hit and for some time felt guilty for not being a missionary."

Smith does not read as much theology as he used to. He now likes to listen to tapes by Dr. Dean Martin, the former pastor of Trinity Methodist University of Florida. His time is spoken for to a large degree by his profession. "I'm not the kind of person who wants two weeks off to do nothing," he said. "I'd rather have a day here and a day there."

There are drawbacks to having one's days crammed so full, though, and this is especially true for a parent. "Most fathers wish they would have spent more time with their children," Smith said, "but a man has to make a choice, and he doesn't always make the right one. The children have turned out well, though. They are not society problems; they are well adjusted and are Christian-oriented. I'd like to think the time I spent with my children as they grew up was quality time. I remember I would come home from practice about eight o'clock, and I made sure before the children went to bed that I had spent 20 minutes with Sharon, Sandy, and Scott. This was 20 minutes each, individual time for them to talk about whatever they wanted. We would have little devotions every night—Sharon, Sandy, Scott, and me—in which we would read some Scripture and talk about it. Of course, I spent other time with the children, and I have done many of the typical things fathers do with their children. We'd go sledding on Saturday mornings and do things like that. I'm no different than anyone. Sometimes I just wish I had more time, especially when the children all grew up so fast. I'm trying to spend much more time with Kristen and Kelly, and I suppose it's because I've seen the other kids grow up before I knew it."

Because of Smith's status as a public figure, it hasn't been easy to go many of the places and to do many of the things that most fathers do with their children. "I probably took my older children to the fair once," he said. "I can't do that now because of all the people who would come up and want to talk or get autographs. We'll be in an airport, and someone will come up and ask for my autograph. I tell my girls that doesn't mean their dad is any more important than somebody else. That's the price you pay."

Music is a pleasure Smith can allow himself even while working at home. His favorite music is jazz. "Once in a while, especially when working on a diagram, I'll throw on something," he said, "mainly Stan Kenton or Count Basie. I don't dislike a lot of the popular music, but I don't like it as much. If some of it is on the car radio while I'm driving, I don't turn it off."

Smith has been labeled a very private person by some writers, but he disagrees with that description. "I don't like to go downtown particularly," he said, "but I'm not a recluse. I have this group of friends I enjoy; they are people who would still be friends if I wasn't a coach. We seldom talk about basketball. I avoid party-type, big-group situations, but I do enjoy doing things with other people."

Among Smith's favorite activities are tennis and golf. His regular golf group sometimes plans outings in advance and makes them family affairs. "I like traveling," Smith said, "and Europe is the most fun of anywhere I go because there are no phone calls there."

Smith has a keen sense of humor, exemplified by his observations on a subject that could easily be sensitive to him—his nose. A target of jokes and caricature artists, the Carolina coach's nose is a part of ACC basketball folklore. Smith once received postcards on a regular basis addressed to Coach Nose, Chapel Hill, North Carolina. "The letters don't really bother me," Smith quipped at the time. "What gripes me is that people know exactly whom to bring them to."

A few years back, Smith suffered some nosebleeds, and it was rumored that he had a blood-pressure problem. The UNC coach shrugged it off publicly, despite the fact that he missed practice for one of only three times in his coaching career. (The other two were for funerals.) The nosebleeds occurred for three days within the span of a week, but they were not the reason Smith stopped smoking. That happened on October 15, 1988. He then added some extra pounds, most of which he has since shed.

Due at least in part to what was believed to be Smith's poor health, sportswriters wrote that he might be considering retirement. A rumor to that effect circulated following the 1988–89 season. But Smith's health has been fine, and he has not thought much about quitting his job. "I always try not to think way ahead," he said. "I take it a day at a time, not a year at a time. As I've said before, if the first day of practice rolls around one fall and I'm not excited, then it will be time to quit." Asked by writers about becoming the all-time winningest college basketball coach, Smith said, "To stay in to break [Adolph] Rupp's record [of 875 career collegiate coaching victories] is ridiculous. That's something I promised I would not be interested in doing. I won't. It would say all the wrong things to stay in to get a record. That won't happen!"

Smith is something of a paradox as a coach. He is a fierce competitor, a person who loves the challenges of an athletic contest and the thrill of trying to win. At the same time, he does not believe that winning is everything; in fact, he has his own definition of winning.

Smith does not judge wins according to the same terms most fans and athletes do. "If we play well," he has said, "and lose score-wise, I like to consider the game a win for us because of our execution and effort. But I get caught up with society, too; I like to win. It still bothers me to lose. It goes the other way, too; if we are on the long end of the score but really play poorly, I feel we have lost, even though a win goes into the record book." A prime example came years ago in a Car-

Winningest Active Division I Men's Basketball Coaches by Victories

(Minimum five years as a head coach; includes record at four-year colleges only)

1. Dean Smith, North Carolina 688
2. Jerry Tarkanian, UNLV 565
3. Don Haskins, Texas-El Paso.....................................563
4. Lefty Driesell, James Madison 560
5. Lou Henson, Illinois 556
6. Norm Stewart, Missouri 552
7. Gene Bartow, Alabama-Birmingham 536
8. Bobby Knight, Indiana 532
9. Glenn Wilkes, Stetson 512
10. Tom Young, Old Dominion 510

Winningest All-Time Division I Men's Basketball Coaches by Victories

(Minimum 10 head-coaching seasons in Division I)

1. Adolph Rupp, Kentucky 875
2. Phog Allen, Kansas 770
3. Henry Iba, Oklahoma State 767
4. Ed Diddle, Western Kentucky....................................759
5. Ray Meyer, DePaul 724
6. Dean Smith, North Carolina 688
7. John Wooden, UCLA...664
8. Ralph Miller, Wichita State, Iowa, Oregon State 657
9. Marv Harshman, Washington State, Washington 642
10. Norman Sloan, the Citadel, N. C. State, Florida 627

michael Auditorium triumph over an opponent reputed to be a pushover. Overconfidence and the visiting team's hunger to upset a nationally ranked foe were to blame for the unexpectedly slim margin of victory. "This game I rate a loss," Smith said afterwards, "because we should not have had so much difficulty winning and because I did not prepare our team well enough. We seemed to take our opponent for granted. The effort is the big thing. If we play hard, the best I think we can, and still lose, then I have to be pleased, regardless of the outcome."

On another occasion, Smith put it this way: "At times, I really have gone back and looked at game film and have seen that we could not have played much better. How can I feel bad about that? I enjoy succeeding and winning, but I take the greatest pride in knowing I did a good job. After a loss, I'm anxious to practice and get going again. The worst losses are the ones which end a season. There's nothing we can do then until the next season. I try to be prepared for anything, but accepting a loss really isn't that difficult. I just have to remember that a game was all that was lost, and that's not the end of the world. I try to remember that basketball is not everything. That takes the emptiness out of defeat and prevents me from being too elated after victory."

Smith's competitiveness is brought out by the biggest games on the Tar Heels' schedule. "The games I like best," he said, "are the ones in which nobody knows who is going to win. Those are the important games, the ones which everyone figures will go down to the final seconds. The only games which bother me are the ones in which we're supposed to win by 25 points. The easiest games are the ones which have us as underdogs."

Although Smith feels that won-lost records are overemphasized, he admits being caught in the undertow at times. "The motivation our coaching staff at North Carolina provides for our players is not to necessarily prove something, but to go out and execute well. To get our players to

Carolina players celebrate
winning the 1977 ACC Tournament

perform as well as they can every night we take the floor—
that is our goal. But I still have trouble with my own beliefs in
this respect. I should be more upset . . . when we play poorly
and win than when we play well and lose. I continue to have
some problems with this way of thinking, even though I feel it
is the correct way. I'm not as much this way as I used to be,
but I have to admit sometimes I feel pretty good when I say,
'Hey, we got by with one,' after playing badly and winning.
Not being upset if we lose after playing well goes back to the
question of goals. I don't think the goal should simply be to
win."

Smith has another reason for minimizing the importance of
victory. "Yes, there is a reason," he said. "My oldest daughter, Sharon, had an emergency tracheotomy when she was 18

months old. That was in 1956, and that was a real crisis. From that time, I have been much better than I was about thinking I just had to win a game. I really am a competitor, but I have been better able to put things into perspective since that time. No basketball game is a true crisis."

Smith realizes, however, that society does not accept his philosophy about winning and losing. "No, society counters what I say. No matter how much I tell our players there is no real pressure to win a game, people on the street, newspapers, television, and radio all oppose that view. As a result, the players feel they have to win. They feel better when someone on campus is patting them on the back because we won a game. Athletics reflect society too much. I get so upset when a man like Bob Spear is not given the credit or recognition he deserves. His won-lost record was not all that outstanding, and although it was above .500, in the world's eyes he just doesn't have the numbers. To me, he was a highly successful coach—always playing the bigger teams and always the underdog, but having amazing success. I suggested to our national coaches' organization that we pick a coach of the year someday without basing our selection on won-lost records. Maybe we would even honor someone with a record under .500, but it would be someone who had done a super job given his situation. The success ethic has gotten out of hand in athletics. The bottom line in business is did your company make money, and I think too much of this is done in United States culture.

"Universities should obviously lead society, not reflect it," Smith said, "but in the athletic world at the college level, we tend to reflect society in general. For example, universities could lead the way by stepping in and saying, 'He's our coach, and we don't care what his record is. We think he has cared about his players, and he has worked hard. He is competent and knows his game, his players graduate, and he is going to remain our coach even if he has six straight losing seasons.' I knew a coach who said once he wasn't going to cheat, but it came down to a situation where that coach had to win in order to keep his job. He wanted to stay in coaching. Now, I'm not going to judge that man, but I will say I think that's where universities have the chance to lead in athletics as they are supposedly leading in presenting new ideas in academics. It is great to see universities try to capture the imagination of students and try to stimulate them to learn and go forward, rather than just teaching the same things which always have been taught. Why can't college presidents step in and do the same in the athletic world? Part of the reason is probably because every college president is a human being who gets a kick out of his team doing well. And the money is always a factor."

Smith put college athletics into perspective. "I don't know whether basketball or football at the level we have them are really all that healthy," he said, "but I think college athletics serve as a common rallying point. They provide a rallying point around which the faculty, the students, the 60-year-old alumnus, and the 28-year-old alumnus can all kind of group together. It helps their self-esteem to say 'We're number one' or 'That's our school.' Maybe those people are not doing as well in their lives to need that kind of self-esteem which comes through athletic programs, but I can still see that we all have pride in our school. So that does add a lot of pressure to coaching. . . .

"The main good thing I can see about athletics at this level, other than the rallying point, is the example which is provided for young people. They can see others working hard toward their goal—they might not reach their goal, but the work helps and might make trying for the goal worthwhile. It's like a musician who practices 14 hours a day but doesn't have the talent to go on. The work put in by that person makes him or her more disciplined. There is discipline practiced on a team of athletes. Our team at North Carolina represents a lot of people, and an image is involved. Some people claim images are phony, but if an image keeps a player from punching someone on national television, then that's not wrong. An example has been set because a player doesn't want to embarrass the university or his teammates."

Smith knows how rampant fans and alumni can become in support of their teams, and he feels their desire to win has swelled to ugly proportions. "Our whole society has that 'We're number one' syndrome, and I think that is bad," he said. "I'm afraid some fans think winning at any cost is fine. I think fans could be asked if they would like to cheat and win a national championship, and many fans, if they were honest, would say yes, they would. That's a shame."

With the extraordinary popularity of sports, athletes and coaches find themselves on a pedestal. Smith feels that fan worship is much overdone. "I laughed at something which happened in Harrisonburg, Virginia, involving Ralph Sampson," Smith said in reference to the seven-foot-four star who was heavily recruited in 1979. "All the people in Virginia, the legislators and even the governor, were saying to Ralph Sampson that he owed it to his state to remain in Virginia. I wondered if they were insisting that the valedictorian of Harrisonburg High also stay in the state. I wondered how many Harrisonburg people even knew the name of that valedictorian. The valedictorian could have gone to MIT or Harvard, and no one would have cared. That's back to a reflection of our society."

Today's interest in college basketball has made coaches' jobs much more difficult than they were when Smith took over as North Carolina's head coach in 1961. "The difference is like night and day in terms of what coaches have to do," he said. "That's why we're overpaid. We were underpaid back then. I didn't have any pressure then, though. Nobody expected us to win anything. And coaches didn't have to do all the things they ask us to do now. The fans and media have placed us in kind of a glass house."

North Carolina's long-running success has catapulted its coach into a position of high visibility, even in the much-publicized Atlantic Coast Conference. It has also triggered

**Ralph Sampson defends against
the Tar Heels' Sam Perkins**

Photo by Hugh Morton

endless comparisons, with each rival coach's success considered a challenge to Smith's reputation as the league's resident genius. Smith himself laughs at such suggestions. "Too much is probably made of coaching, period," he said. "In the ACC, we hear all that about coaching rivalries, but we don't play one-on-one. I think there is too much of that talk."

Of the notion that Duke Coach Mike Krzyzewski has stolen some of his thunder in the ACC, Smith said, "We at Carolina certainly give Mike more than a second thought, but it's not a personal thing. No, I'm not really worried about my reputation or losing ground to him. Duke has a tremendous program, but so did Virginia with [Ralph] Sampson and so did State when Norm [Sloan] had David Thompson. I never pay any attention to what people are saying or writing about me. I like to know what I think about me and not what others are thinking. I'm not saying I don't care, because I do. Everyone wants to be liked. Every coach wants to be respected by his players, and I'm no different. People say I'm modest, but I'm not so much modest as I'm realistic. . . .

"I try to enter each new season with a completely open mind," Smith said of his philosophy of giving his athletes a fair chance to earn playing time. "I never want to have my mind made up like I used to. If you say to yourself, 'Well, next year we're going to have so-and-so here and this guy over there,' then there is a tendency to play those people. If I did that, there would never be any Darrell Elston stories. Darrell was the 13th man on our squad at the end of his sophomore year in 1972. I wasn't sure how much he would play and told him so. I even told him perhaps he would want to look at another school. But he said, 'No, I like it at Carolina, and I want to work hard and see what happens.' He ended up all-ACC by his senior year and played three years of pro ball in the ABA. Seeing this kind of improvement is one of the thrills of fall practices, and I really get excited every year when it's time to start again."

One of his tasks is to motivate, but Smith believes that

Active Coaches
with Six or More 25-Win Seasons
At the Division I Level

Dean Smith, North Carolina 17
Jerry Tarkanian, UNLV 12
Jim Boeheim, Syracuse 8
John Thompson, Georgetown 6
Denny Crum, Louisville 6
Norm Stewart, Missouri 6

All-Time Leaders
in NCAA Regional Championships

John Wooden UCLA 12
Dean Smith, North Carolina 7
Denny Crum, Louisville 6
Adolph Rupp, Kentucky 6
Guy Lewis, Houston 5
Harold Olsen, Ohio State 4
Henry Iba, Oklahoma State 4
Jack Gardner, Utah and Kansas State 4
Bobby Knight, Indiana 4
Fred Taylor, Ohio State 4

Active Coaches with Four
or More NCAA Regional Championships

Dean Smith 7
Denny Crum 6
Bobby Knight 4

aspect of his coaching duties may be overrated. "Certainly, trying to motivate is our job as coaches to a degree, but I think there are very many self-motivators at this level of athletics," Smith said. "They have already spent hours, many hours, working at the game of basketball, and they have some goals in mind. So in most cases, we have little motivating to do. It's our belief that if a player comes to North Carolina, he's going to try hard, or he'll feel he is the one who is out of step."

There is no off-season program at Carolina. "But we do tell our players what they should work on during the summer," Smith said, "and it's just understood that they're going to work on their game."

A coach's effectiveness in motivating his players may also be influenced by outside factors. "Sometimes, I think a coach thinks he may have more control over his team than he does," Smith said. "We really don't have that much control. Like a player's frame of mind about a game, for instance. Sometime during the day of a game, some student may say to one of our players, 'Oh, you're going to kill these guys by 25 points tonight.' The players start believing things like that, and then we're in trouble. I don't know how much control I actually have over our team."

Asked about the things for which he would most like to be remembered, Smith said, "It's fun to come up with new ideas. The screen at the point of the ball, our scramble, and others— they are my ideas which have been adopted by others. Those kind of things would be nice to be remembered for, things which contributed to basketball. I'm very proud of any contribution I have been able to make to the game of basketball. But some of the things we have come up with at Carolina were at least partly a result of accidents. The way we run four corners was. The foul-line huddle started in practice. All of our players knew what we were doing offensively and defensively, so some of our players began huddling so other players they were scrimmaging couldn't hear what they were planning to do. Then we started doing it in games. We didn't say, 'Hey,

Darrell Elston

let's do that huddle thing in a game.' It just happened. The beauty of the game is what I think is so great. In some way, if an idea or two or three—if you could see it out there wherever teams are playing basketball—that would be nice. It would also be good to be remembered for having players who graduated."

The figure 97.7 percent is called the "bottom line" in UNC's basketball media guide. It represents the graduation rate of Smith's players, and it is the number that really matters. Every player who has stayed in school and played four years under Smith has received a degree.

In looking back to his hiring as the University of North Carolina's head basketball coach in 1961, Smith reflected, "I'm just trying to do what Chancellor Aycock told me to do at that time—have our players graduate and do it within the rules."

Doing things the right way has been the only way for Smith. It's easy to see why his program is considered a measuring stick for college basketball.

One of the richest of compliments is to say that a person is unchanged by success. Those who know Smith best say he is the same man who was a substitute guard on the Kansas University basketball team and an assistant coach at the Air Force Academy. Smith has matured, with new wrinkles in his game plan and specks of gray in his hair, but his character and compassion have stayed intact. He remains more concerned that players receive their diplomas than that trophies jam his glass case.

Smith's fondest memories are not only of particular games or special victories. "When a player of ours goes on and does well in any field, that makes me feel especially good," he said. "No one game really stands out, although there have been some exciting ones. The tournament means so much in the ACC. It used to mean everything as far as getting into the NCAAs, and so I suppose the first ACC Tournament we won sticks out in my mind. It was a great satisfaction to win both the regular season and tournament in 1967, as those were my

Dean Smith and the Tar Heels

first times experiencing such things since I became the Carolina coach. I can remember my first game as head coach [an 80–46 Tar Heel win over Virginia] and our first win at Kentucky [in the 1962–63 season]. Kentucky always has had great teams, and of course Adolph Rupp was such a wonderful coach. We had just been defeated by Indiana at Bloomington, and our players got together and said they wouldn't be beaten. This game was at Kentucky, where Coach Rupp's teams had only lost 13 times in 25 years. We went in there and won, and that meant a lot. Wins away from home have always been special, as have those against rivals and formidable opposition. I don't have a favorite of all the teams we've had at Carolina; I've been really happy with all the years we've had. I can't think of any year I thought to myself, 'Oh, gosh, I'll be glad when this season is over.' I've never felt that way."

Smith doesn't second-guess himself. "I'm really not one to look back," he said. "This year, I'm glad I'm 59 years old. I don't wish I was starting college again, and I don't wish this or that. I am happy with today and try to do the most with it I possibly can. I'm very lucky. How many people can look forward to going to work? I do. I'm a very happy man. I haven't had much tragedy in my life at all; I've really had a lot of good things come my way. I just look forward to each day, and I think about next season next year and not before. There is no pressure to win any certain number of games each season or to continue what we have done in past seasons, because those are in the past. Each season is a new one, and each team has a different identity. That is one of the things which makes coaching in college fun—to see how different guys react with each other."

As for his own achievements, Smith said, "My greatest coaching job depends on our players and how well they get along. I don't think of any particular season in terms of my own coaching success. As for my proudest achievement, I guess it's that I still have my job.

"I don't like to talk about my coaching so much," Smith said. "Every coach is trying to find a new way. We all seek a better way to play the game. Necessity has a way of producing ideas. Lots of things which happen are the results of other ideas which didn't work out. There are many, many fine coaches in basketball today, and they are bringing a lot of good ideas into the game. The ACC has outstanding coaches, and there are good ones everywhere."

Though Smith is looked upon as the patriarch of Carolina basketball, he claims that his influence is exaggerated. "I think it's preposterous to think I shape the character of players," he said. "We are a family and we talk about things, but I don't dwell on getting my views across. Their good character traits are learned from their own families."

The close relationship Smith enjoys with his players has provided him his greatest pleasure as a coach. That is why he stays in touch with them. That is also why he has no plans for lengthy vacations or afternoons spent on the porch languidly reliving the good old days. "I have no idea how long I'll go on," he said. "If I coached the same team for 15 years, the players would get tired of hearing my voice, and I would get tired of seeing the same mistakes. But that's the nice thing about coaching in college—there is a new group coming in each fall. In a way, I get a fresh start every year. As long as I enjoy what I'm doing, why should I change or quit? Sometimes, following a season which has been drawn out with all the games and travel, I can't imagine being excited about next season's first practice coming again. But after a little time away, I start thinking about the players who will be on our squad, and I become eager all over again. I realize I'm extremely fortunate to have a job like this."

Smith has established an outstanding tradition. He has proven himself an innovator, a crafty strategist, and a smooth operator in the heat of battle. He has left an indelible stamp on college basketball and on the lives of the young men who have played for him.

Dean Smith has been much more than a coach.

CAROLINA LETTERMEN UNDER DEAN SMITH

A Summary of the Lettermen

Total Number of Lettermen under Smith.............................172
Lettermen Who Have Graduated......................................168
Number Who Have Done Graduate Work...............................75
Number Who Have Played Pro Basketball in the NBA or ABA.........38
Number Who Have Played Pro Basketball Overseas or in the CBA.....31

The 172 lettermen now reside in 24 states, the District of Columbia, and six foreign countries.

Present Occupations of the 172 Lettermen

Students Currently in Graduate School 10
   (Four in medicine and six in other fields)
Attorneys...14
Doctors...11
   (Six doctors and five dentists)
Businessmen...83
Coaches and Teachers..29
   (14 in high school, 13 in college, and two in the professional ranks)
Professional Basketball...16
   (12 in the NBA, four in Europe)
Officers in the Armed Forces 3
Pastors 2
Recreation Departments 2
Others...2

Class of '62

Peppy Callahan
Degree: AB (Education–Math)
Graduate Work: MAT (Math) '64
Present Position: Col., U.S. Air Force, Commander, 6th ACCS (TAC), Langley AFB, VA

Hugh Donohue
Degree: AB (Arts and Sciences–History/Education)
Present Position: Real Estate, Durham, NC

Jim Hudock
Degree: BS (Ind. Rel.)
Graduate Work: DDS '68
Present Position: Dentist, Kinston, NC

Harry Jones
Degree: AB (Philosophy)
Graduate Work: MA (Philosophy) '63
Present Position: Teacher, Lansing, NC

Don Walsh
Degree: BA (Pol. Sci.)
Graduate Work: JD (Law) '65
Present Position: President, Indiana Pacers, NBA

Class of '63

*Larry Brown
Degree: AB (History)
Present Position: Head Coach, San Antonio Spurs, NBA

Charles Burns
Degree: AB (Sociology)
Present Position: Sales Rep., Levi
    Strauss, Lexington, KY

Dieter Krause
Degree: AB (Rec. Admin.)
Present Position: Lt. Col., U.S.
    Army, West Germany

Yogi Poteet
Degree: AB (Sociology)
Graduate Work: MAT (Sociology)
    '65
Present Position: School Dean,
    U.S. Army, Logistics Mgt.
    College, Ft. Lee, VA

Richard Vinroot
Degree: BS (Bus. Admin.)
Graduate Work: JD (Law) '66
Present Position: Attorney,
    Charlotte, NC

Eddie Burke, Mgr.
Degree: BS (Ind. Rel.)
Present Position: Senior Marketing
    Rep., IBM Corp., Wilmington,
    NC

Art Katz
Degree: AB (Education)
Graduate Work: MAT (Education)
    '67
Present Position: High School
    Teacher and Health Specialist,
    Wayne, NJ

Bryan McSweeney
Degree: AB (Pol. Sci.)
Graduate Work: MBA (Prof. Mgt.)
    '75
Present Position: Vice-President
    and Branch Mgr., Fitzgerald,
    Dearman, and Roberts, Irvine,
    CA

Charles Shaffer
Degree: AB (History)
Graduate Work: JD (Law) '67
Present Position: Attorney,
    Atlanta, GA

Elliott Nurnick, Mgr.
Degree: AB (Pol. Sci.)
Present Position: Sports Promotion
    and Nightclub Owner, Raleigh,
    NC

Class of '64

Bruce Bowers
Degree: BA (History)
Graduate Work: Financial Services
    '83
Present Position: Senior Trust and
    Investment Officer, Quincy
    Savings Bank, Quincy, MA

Mike Cooke
Degree: AB (English)
Present Position: Sales, Hartwell
    Mgt. Co., Hartwell, GA

Class of '65

Bill Brown
Degree: AB (History)
Graduate Work: JD (Law) '68
Present Position: Attorney,
    Atlanta, GA

*Billy Cunningham
Degree: AB (History)
Present Position: Executive Vice-
    President, Financial Printing,
    Pandick Press, Philadelphia, PA;
    Executive Vice-President, Miami
    Heat, NBA

Bill Galantai
Degree: AB (History)
Graduate Work: MA and Ph.D.
(Education) '72 and '76
Present Position: Teacher, New
York City Schools, Baldwin
Harbor, NY

Pud Hassell
Degree: AB (History)
Graduate Work: JD (Law) '68
Present Position: Attorney,
Raleigh, NC

Ray Respess
Degree: BS (Ind. Rel.)
Present Position: Dir. of Admin.
Services, Caswell Training
Center, Kinston, NC

Terry Ronner
Degree: BS (Bus. Admin.)
Present Position: Vice-President,
Carolina Treet, Inc.,
Wilmington, NC

Mike Smith
Degree: BS (Math)
Present Position: Manager, Indiana
Bell, Indianapolis, IN

Class of '66

Bob Bennett
Degree: AB (Pol. Sci.)
Graduate Work: JD (Law) '69
Present Position: Attorney, Los
Angeles, CA

Bill Harrison
Degree: BA (Economics)
Graduate Work: MBA (Bus.
Admin.) '67, Harvard Business
School, SMP Program '79
Present Position: Exec. Vice-
President, Chemical Bank, New
York, NY

Ray Hassell
Degree: AB (History)
Present Position: Financial
Counselor and Registered
Investment Advisor, Cigna
Financial Services, Marietta, GA

Mike Conte
(formerly Iannarella)
Degree: AB (English)
Graduate Work: MA (English) '67
Present Position: Numismatist,
Sharon Hills, PA

Earl Johnson
Degree: BS (Pol. Sci.)
Graduate Work: DDS '70
Present Position: Dentist, Raleigh,
NC

Jim Moore
Degree: AB (Psychology)
Graduate Work: Psychology '67
Present Position: Insurance Exec.,
Wilmington, NC

Jim Smithwick
Degree: BS (Chemistry)
Graduate Work: MD '70
Present Position: Pediatrician,
Laurinburg, NC

John Yokley
Degree: BS (Ind. Rel.)
Present Position: Vice-President,
Universal Furniture Industries,
Inc., High Point, NC

Joe Youngblood, Mgr.
Degree: BA (Pol. Sci.)
Present Position: President,
Fletcher Auto Agency,
Asheville, NC

Class of '67

Tom Gauntlett
Degree: AB (Pol. Sci.)
Graduate Work: Law (1 year)
Present Position: President and
   CEO, Precision Color, Dallas,
   PA

*Bob Lewis
Degree: AB (Rec. Admin.)
Present Position: John F. Kennedy
   Center for Culture, Washington,
   DC

Mark Mirken
Degree: BA (Pol. Sci.)
Graduate Work: JD (Law) '70
Present Position: President, M and
   M Assoc. (Shopping Center
   Developer), Boston, MA

Donnie Moe
Degree: BS (Bus. Admin.)
Present Position: Vice-
   President/Gen. Mgr., Martin-
   Marietta Aggregates,
   Greensboro, NC

**Ian Morrison
Degree: BS (Education)
Graduate Work: MSW '74
Present Position: Teacher and
   Coach, Kingsport, TN

Bill Cochrane, Mgr.
Degree: AB (Education)
Graduate Work: MA (Education)
   '68
Present Position: High School
   Teacher and Coach, Virginia
   Beach, VA

Fred Emmerson, Mgr.
Degree: BA (English)
Graduate Work: JD (Law) '72
Present Position: Attorney,
   Winston-Salem, NC

Ben Thompson, Mgr.
Degree: BA (English)
Graduate Work: DDS '71, MS '73
Present Position: Dentist,
   Winston-Salem, NC

Class of '68

Greg Campbell
Degree: BS (Bus. Admin.)
Present Position: Vice-President,
   Financial Services, Rex Hospital,
   Raleigh, NC

Ralph Fletcher
Degree: BS (Bus. Admin.)
Graduate Work: MBA (Bus.
   Admin.) '69
Present Position: Investment
   Banking, Saloman Brothers,
   New York, NY

Jim Frye
Degree: BA (Psychology)
Graduate Work: MA (Education)
   '80, Law (1 year)
Present Position: Dean of
   Students, Orland Park, IL

Dickson Gribble, Jr.
Degree: BS (Chemistry)
Graduate Work: MBA (Bus.
   Admin.) '78
Present Position: Lt. Col., U.S.
   Army, Representative to the
   Director, National Security
   Agency Fellowship Program,
   Columbia, MD

*Larry Miller
Degree: BS (Bus. Admin.)
Present Position: President, Larry
   Miller and Associates Real
   Estate, Raleigh, NC

Class of '69

**Jim Bostick
Degree: ALA, BA
Graduate Work: MS (Biomed. Eng.) '81
Present Position: Coordinator of Academic Computing and Coach, Durham, NC

Joe Brown
Degree: BS (Bus. Admin.)
Present Position: Vice-President, Mortgage Loans and Real Estate, Durham Life, Raleigh, NC

*Bill Bunting
Degree: AB (Education)
Present Position: Banker, First Federal Savings and Loan Assoc. of Raleigh, Raleigh, NC

Franklin "Rusty" Clark
Degree: AB (Zoology)
Graduate Work: MD '73
Present Position: General/Vascular Surgeon, Fayetteville, NC

*Dick Grubar
Degree: BS (Bus. Admin.)
Present Position: Vice-President, Weaver Companies, Greensboro, NC

Gerald Tuttle
Degree: BA (Phys. Ed.)
Present Position: President, Classic Leather, Inc., Hickory, NC

Bob Coleman, Mgr.
Degree: BA (Rec. Admin.)
Graduate Work: MS (Rec. Admin.) '74
Present Position: Owner/Distributor, Thomas Built Buses, Columbia, SC

Randy Forehand, Mgr.
Degree: BA (Zoology)
Graduate Work: MD '74
Present Position: Pediatric Allergist and Asst. Professor of Pediatrics, Philadelphia, PA

Class of '70

Jim Delany
Degree: AB (Pol. Sci.)
Graduate Work: JD (Law) '73
Present Position: Commissioner, Big Ten Conference, Schaumburg, IL

Eddie Fogler
Degree: BA (Math)
Graduate Work: MAT (Education) '72
Present Position: Head Basketball Coach, Vanderbilt University, Nashville, TN

*Charles Scott
Degree: AB (History)
Present Position: President, Gentleman's Footgear, Atlanta, GA

Ricky Webb
Degree: AB (Chemistry)
Graduate Work: DDS '73
Present Position: Periodontist/Real Estate, New Bern, NC

Gra Whitehead
Degree: BS (Bus. Admin.)
Present Position: President, Grasunan Farm, Scotland Neck, NC

Leroy Upperman, Mgr.
Degree: BA (History)
Graduate Work: JD (Law) '73
Present Position: Attorney, Los Angeles, CA

Class of '71

+**Dave Chadwick**
Degree: BA (RTVMP)
Graduate Work: Ed.S. '76, D.Min. '80
Present Position: Senior Pastor, Forest Hill Presbyterian Church, Charlotte, NC

Lee Dedmon
Degree: AB (Rec. Admin.)
Graduate Work: MA (Education) '76
Present Position: Principal, Highland Junior High School, Gastonia, NC

Don Eggleston
Degree: AB (Pol. Sci.)
Graduate Work: JD (Law) '74
Present Position: Attorney, Greensboro, NC

Dale Gipple
Degree: BA (Pol. Sci.)
Present Position: Sales Rep., Nike Shoe Co., Raleigh, NC

Richard Tuttle
Degree: BS (Rec. Admin.)
Present Position: Asst. Dir., Parks and Recreation, Gastonia, NC

Ben Reid, Mgr.
Degree: AB (History)
Graduate Work: JD (Law) '74
Present Position: Attorney, Miami, FL

Class of '72

*****Bill Chamberlain**
Degree: BA (Gen. Studies)
Present Position: Sales, Bob Barbour BMW-Jeep-Volvo, Greenville, NC

Billy Chambers
Degree: AB (Chemistry)
Graduate Work: DDS '76, MS '79
Present Position: Pediatric Dental Specialist, Asheville, NC

+**Craig Corson**
Degree: BA (Psychology)
Graduate Work: MBA (Bus. Admin.) '83, Ed.D. (Counseling) '90
Present Position: Doctoral Student, UNC-Greensboro, Greensboro, NC

Mike Earey
Degree: BS (Bus. Admin.)
Present Position: Bank Officer, Central Carolina Bank, Wilmington, NC

+**Kim Huband**
Degree: AB (English)
Graduate Work: MS (Rec. Admin.) '76
Present Position: Park and Recreation Planner, Dept. of Natural Resources and Community Dev., Raleigh, NC

*****Steve Previs**
Degree: BA (RTVMP)
Present Position: Equities Trader and Technical Analyst, Manama, Bahrain

*****Dennis Wuycik**
Degree: AB (Economics)
Present Position: President, DMW Enterprises, Chapel Hill, NC

Jon Barrett, Mgr.
Degree: BA (Pol. Sci.)
Graduate Work: JD (Law) '78
Present Position: Attorney, Charlotte, NC

Class of '73

John Austin
Degree: BS (Ind. Rel.)
Deceased

John Cox
Degree: BA (Psychology)
Graduate Work: M.Ed. (Education) '75
Present Position: Teacher and Businessman, Durham, NC

+Donn Johnston
Degree: BA (Pol. Sci.)
Graduate Work: JD (Law) '80
Present Position: Attorney, Philadelphia, PA

*George Karl
Degree: BS (Pol. Sci.)
Present Position: Head Coach, Real Madrid Basketball Team, Madrid, Spain

+*Robert McAdoo
Degree: AB (Sociology)
Present Position: Pro Basketball, Milan Tracers, Italy

Doug Donald, Mgr.
Degree: BS (Ind. Rel./Pol. Sci.)
Present Position: Presand Industrial Supply Co., Leland, NC

Class of '74

*Darrell Elston
Degree: BA (History)
Graduate Work: Accounting '82
Present Position: Materials Mgt., GM/Delco, Inc., Kokomo, IN

Ray Hite
Degree: BS (Education)
Graduate Work: ME (Education) '75
Present Position: Asst. Vice-President, Carey Winston Realtors, Chevy Chase, MD

*Bobby Jones
Degree: BA (Psychology)
Present Position: Athletic Dir., Charlotte Christian School, Charlotte, NC

+John O'Donnell
Degree: BA (Psychology/Pol. Sci.)
Graduate Work: MD '80
Present Position: Orthopedic Surgeon, Baltimore, MD

Greg Miles, Mgr.
Degree: BA (Pol. Sci.)
Present Position: Blackwell Brothers, Inc., Burlington, NC

Class of '75

Mickey Bell
Degree: BS (Business)
Present Position: Vice-President of Sales, Converse, Inc., North Reading, MA

Ray Harrison
Degree: AB (Rec. Admin.)
Present Position: Olympic Chemical Co., Greensboro, NC

+Brad Hoffman
Degree: BS (Bus. Admin.)
Present Position: Manufacturers Rep., Classic Leather/St. Timothy Chair Co., Columbus, OH

+**Ed Stahl**
Degree: BS (Business)
Present Position: Account Exec.,
  Executive Adventures, Inc.,
  Raleigh, NC

Charles Waddell
Degree: BS (Ind. Rel.)
Graduate Work: MBA '84
Present Position: Vice-President,
  NCNB, Charlotte, NC

+*Donald Washington
Degree: AB (Studio Art)
Present Position: President, The
  Washington Corp., Montpellier,
  France

John Rancke, Mgr.
Degree: BS (Rec. Admin.)
Present Position: Sales, Galaxy
  Homes, Jonesboro, GA

Class of '76

*Bill Chambers
Degree: AB (Psychology)
Graduate Work: Education '83
Present Position: Head Basketball
  Coach, North Carolina Wesleyan
  College, Rocky Mount, NC

Dave Hanners
Degree: BA (Education)
Graduate Work: MA (Education)
  '78
Present Position: Asst. Basketball
  Coach, University of North
  Carolina, Chapel Hill, NC

*Mitch Kupchak
Degree: BA (Pol. Sci./Psychology)
Graduate Work: MBA '87
Present Position: Asst. Gen. Mgr.,
  Los Angeles Lakers, NBA

Tony Shaver
Degree: BS (Business)
Graduate Work: MAT (Social
  Studies) '83
Present Position: Head Basketball
  Coach, Hampden-Sydney
  College, Hampden-Sydney, VA

Dan Veazey, Mgr.
Degree: BA (History)
Graduate Work: MD '81
Present Position: Physician,
  Hendersonville, NC

Class of '77

+**Bruce Buckley**
Degree: BA (Math)
Graduate Work: JD (Law) '81
Present Position: Attorney,
  Charlotte, NC

Woody Coley
Degree: BA (Economics)
Present Position: Real Estate
  Developer, Orlando, FL

*Walter Davis
Degree: AB (Rec. Admin.)
Present Position: Pro Basketball,
  Denver Nuggets, NBA

*John Kuester
Degree: AB (Education)

+*Tommy LaGarde
Degree: BA (Economics)
Present Position: Investments,
  New York, NY

**James Smith
Degree: BA (Humanities)
Graduate Work: MA (Education) '79
Deceased

Class of '78

*Geff Crompton
Degree: AB (Rec. Admin.)
Present Position: Management, Pizza Hut Corp., Tallahassee, FL

*Phil Ford
Degree: AB (Business)
Present Position: Asst. Basketball Coach, University of North Carolina, Chapel Hill, NC

*Tom Zaliagiris
Degree: AB (Education)
Present Position: Gen. Mgr., Statesville Chair Co., Conover, NC

John Cohen, Mgr.
Degree: BS (History)
Present Position: President, Carlyle and Co. Jewelers, Greensboro, NC

Jeff Mason, Mgr.
Degree: AB (Journalism)
Graduate Work: JD (Law) '83
Present Position: Asst. Counsel, USLICO Corp., Arlington, VA

Class of '79

*Dudley Bradley
Degree: AB (Sociology/Recreation)

Ged Doughton
Degree: AB (Pol. Sci.)
Present Position: Vice-President, First Charlotte Corp., Charlotte, NC

**Loren Lutz
Degree: BA (Phys. Ed.)
Present Position: High School Teacher and Asst. Basketball Coach, Denver, CO

**Keith Valentine
Degree: AB (Rec. Admin.)
Present Position: Computer Operator, Heilig-Meyers, Richmond, VA

+Randy Wiel
Degree: AB (Education)
Graduate Work: MS (Education) '87
Present Position: Asst. Basketball Coach and Phys. Ed. Instructor, University of North Carolina, Chapel Hill, NC

Rick Duckett, Mgr.
Degree: AB (Education)
Graduate Work: MS (Education) '80
Present Position: Asst. Basketball Coach, Wichita State University, Wichita, KS

Class of '80

Dave Colescott
Degree: AB (Education)
Present Position: District Mgr., Midwest Sales, Hanes Corp., Cleveland, OH

*Mike O'Koren
Degree: AB (Rec. Admin.)
Present Position: Broadcaster, New Jersey Nets, NBA

+**Steve Krafcisin
Degree: BS (Rec. Admin.)
Graduate Work: ME (Phys. Ed.) '82
Present Position: Asst. Basketball Coach, Iowa State University, Ames, IA

+John Virgil
Degree: BA (Rec. Admin.)
Present Position: Sara Lee Corp., PYA-Monarch Co., Atlanta, GA

+**Jeff Wolf**
Degree: AB (Pol. Sci.)
Present Position: Marketing Mgr.,
    Accutech Computer Systems
    Ltd., Sheboygan, WI

+*****Rich Yonakor**
Degree: BA (Rec. Admin.)
Present Position: Senior
    Programmer Analyst, Sara Lee
    Corp., Winston-Salem, NC

Kenny Lee, Mgr.
Degree: BS (Business)
Present Position: Businessman,
    Raleigh, NC

Class of '81

+**Pete Budko**
Degree: AB (Physics)
Present Position: Investment
    Banker, NCNB, Charlotte, NC

Eric Kenny
Degree: BA (Chemistry)
Graduate Work: MD '85
Present Position: Chief Medical
    Resident, Medical College of
    Virginia, Richmond, VA

+**Mike Pepper**
Degree: AB (Ind. Rel.)
Present Position: Leasing Agent,
    Continental Development
    Corp., McLean, VA

*****Al Wood**
Degree: AB (Rec. Admin.)
Present Position: Pro Basketball,
    Europe

Lindsay Reed, Mgr.
Degree: BS (Ind. Rel.)
Graduate Work: M.Div. (1 year),
    Teacher Certification '92
Present Position: Graduate
    Student, Millersville University,
    Millersville, PA

Class of '82

+**Jeb Barlow**
Degree: BS (Business)
Present Position: Sales, Standard
    Oxygen Service, Little Rock, AR

*****Jimmy Black**
Degree: BA (RTVMP)
Present Position: Asst. Basketball
    Coach, University of South
    Carolina

*****Chris Brust**
Degree: AB (Rec. Admin.)
Present Position: Marketing Rep.,
    Trans Title of North Carolina,
    Inc., Salisbury, NC

David Daly, Mgr.
Degree: BA (RTVMP)
Present Position: Photographer,
    WBTV-TV, Charlotte, NC

Chuck Duckett, Mgr.
Degree: BA (History/Pol. Sci.)
Present Position: Investment
    Broker, Scott and Stringfellow,
    Inc., Winston-Salem, NC

Class of '83

+**Jim Braddock**
Degree: BA (Psychology)
Present Position: Teacher and
    Coach, St. Matthews School,
    Jacksonville, FL

*****James Worthy**
Degree: AB (Rec. Admin.)
Present Position: Pro Basketball,
    Los Angeles Lakers, NBA

Julie Dalton Loos, Mgr.
Degree: AB
    (Journalism/Psychology)
Present Position: Copywriter,
    TBWA, St. Louis, MO

Ralph Meekins, Mgr.
Degree: BA (Psychology/Phys. Ed.)
Graduate Work: JD (Law) '86
Present Position: Attorney, Raleigh, NC

Joe Stroman, Mgr.
Degree: AB (Phys. Ed.)
Present Position: Firefighter, Gastonia Fire Dept., Gastonia, NC

Class of '84

Matt Doherty
Degree: BS (Business)
Present Position: Asst. Basketball Coach, Davidson College, Davidson, NC

+Cecil Exum
Degree: BA (Rec. Admin.)
Present Position: Pro Basketball and Dir. of Junior Basketball, Victoria, Australia

Timo Makkonen
Degree: BS (Bus. Admin.)
Graduate Work: MBA '86
Present Position: Hotel Account Mgr., Hyatt Hotels Corp., Chicago, IL

*Sam Perkins
Degree: BA (RTVMP)
Present Position: Pro Basketball, Dallas Mavericks, NBA

David Hart, Mgr.
Degree: BA (Economics), BS (Bus. Admin.)
Present Position: Banking Officer, Wachovia Bank and Trust Co., Asheville, NC

Holly Jones, Mgr.
Degree: BA (Public Policy Analysis)
Graduate Work: M.Div. '87
Present Position: Missionary, Italy

Class of '85

*Michael Jordan
Degree: BA (Geography)
Present Position: Pro Basketball, Chicago Bulls, NBA

Cliff Morris
Degree: BS (Biology)
Graduate Work: MD '89
Present Position: Medical Resident, UNC Hospitals, Chapel Hill, NC

+Buzz Peterson
Degree: BA (Geography)
Present Position: Asst. Basketball Coach, North Carolina State University, Raleigh, NC

**Lynwood Robinson
Degree: BS (Communications)
Present Position: Consumer Credit Consultant, Raleigh, NC

Gary Roper
Degree: BA (Chemistry)
Graduate Work: MD '89
Present Position: Medical Resident, UNC Hospitals, Chapel Hill, NC

**Dean Shaffer
Degree: BS (Social Science)
Present Position: Sales Rep., Kenan Transport, Tampa, FL

Dean McCord, Mgr.
Degree: BA (Chemistry)
Graduate Work: Ph.D. (Pathology)
  '91
Present Position: Graduate
  Student, University of North
  Carolina, Chapel Hill, NC

Jane Snead-Simms, Mgr.
Degree: BS (Math)
Present Position: Software
  Designer, Bell Northern
  Research, Research Triangle
  Park, NC

Class of '86

+John Brownlee**
Degree: BA (Psychology)
Present Position: Leasing Dir.,
  Dallas/Ft. Worth Airport,
  Dallas, TX

***Brad Daugherty**
Degree: BA (RTVMP)
Present Position: Pro Basketball,
  Cleveland Cavaliers, NBA

James Daye
Degree: AB (Education/English)
Present Position: Teacher and
  Head Basketball Coach,
  Northeastern High School,
  Elizabeth City, NC

+Steve Hale
Degree: BA (Biology)
Graduate Work: MD '91
Present Position: Medical Student,
  University of North Carolina,
  Chapel Hill, NC

+*Warren Martin
Degree: BA (History/Geography)
Graduate Work: Teacher
  Certification (Education) '88
Present Position: Teacher, Chapel
  Hill-Carrboro city schools,
  Chapel Hill, NC

Mark Isley, Mgr.
Degree: BA (Education)
Present Position: Asst. Basketball
  Coach, Eastern Randolph High
  School, Ramseur, NC

Lannie Parrish, Mgr.
Degree: BA (Economics)
Present Position: Financial
  Advisor, Fidelity Investments,
  Dallas, TX

Class of '87

+Curtis Hunter
Degree: BA (African Studies)
Present Position: Pro Basketball,
  Australia

Michael Norwood
Degree: BA (Economics)
Present Position: Credit Mgr.,
  Norwest Financial, Richmond,
  VA

+*David Popson
Degree: BA (Geography)
Present Position: Pro Basketball,
  Europe

***Kenny Smith**
Degree: BA (Ind. Rel.)
Present Position: Pro Basketball,
  Atlanta Hawks, NBA

***Joe Wolf**
Degree: BA (Ind. Rel.)
Present Position: Pro Basketball,
  Los Angeles Clippers, NBA

Jan Baldwin, Mgr.
Degree: AB (Math/Education)
Graduate Work: MA (Education
  Admin. Supervision) '90
Present Position: Graduate
  Student, University of North
  Carolina, Chapel Hill, NC

Adam Fleishman, Mgr.
Degree: BS (Bus. Admin.)
Graduate Work: MBA '91
Present Position: Graduate
Student, University of North
Carolina, Chapel Hill, NC

Class of '88

Joe Jenkins
Degree: BA (Biology)
Present Position: President,
Jenkins Construction, Elizabeth
City, NC

+Ranzino Smith
Degree: AB (Afro-American
Studies)
Present Position: Dept. of
Transportation, Raleigh, NC

Mike Ellis, Mgr.
Degree: AB (Education)
Present Position: Asst. Basketball
Coach and Graduate Student,
Virginia Commonwealth
University, Richmond, VA

Kendria Parsons, Mgr.
Degree: BA (International Studies)
Present Position: Management,
Squid's Restaurant, Chapel Hill,
NC

Class of '89

*Steve Bucknall
Degree: AB (RTVMP)

*Jeff Lebo
Degree: BS (Bus. Admin.)
Present Position: Asst. Basketball
Coach, East Tennessee State
University, Johnson City, TN

David May
Degree: BS (Chemistry)
Graduate Work: MD '93
Present Position: Medical Student,
University of North Carolina,
Chapel Hill, NC

Michael Burch, Mgr.
Degree: BA (Economics/Ind. Rel.)
Graduate Work: Master's Program
(Sports Mgt.) '91
Present Position: Graduate Asst.
and Graduate Student, Georgia
Southern College, Statesboro,
GA

*Have played professional basketball in the NBA or ABA

+Have played professional basketball in the Continental Basketball Association, with Athletes in Action, or in Europe, South America, or Australia

**Degree at another university

Information courtesy of the 1989–90 University of North Carolina Basketball Media Guide and the university's Sports Information Office.